PRACTICAL APPROACH TO RESEARCH METHODOLOGY

PRACTICAL APPROACH TO RESEARCH METHODOLOGY

Practical Approach to

Research Methodology

Dr. S.P. Verma
M.Sc., M.Phil.., Ph.D.

AKANSHA PUBLISHING HOUSE
NEW DELHI - 110 059 (INDIA)

AKANSHA PUBLISHING HOUSE
R-37-B, Vani Vihar
Uttam Nagar
New Delhi - 110 059

Showroom
4679/21-B, Ansari Road
Daryaganj, New Delhi - 110 002
Phones: 9811582579, 9212065579

Practical Approach to Research Methodology

First Published. 2005
Reprint–2006
Reprint : 2007

PRINTED IN INDIA

Published by M.P. Misra for Akansha Publishing House, New Delhi - 110 059 and Printed at Tarun Offset Press, Delhi.

Contents

Preface *vii*

1. Research Problem 1
2. Selection of the Research Subject 19
3. Hypothesis 23
4. Designing Research 41
5. Sample Design 83
6. Research Tools 94
7. Interview Schedules 121
8. Data Collection for Social Research: Nature & Purpose 153
9. Interpretation and Analysis of Data 184
10. Related Literature 230
11. Writing Research Proposals: Technique & Guidelines 250

Select Bibliography 263

Index 266

Preface

Research is a systematic investigation to establish facts or principles or to collect information on a subject. Sometimes a novice researcher mistake it as criticism. Criticism is the act of making analysis or evaluation of a work of art or literature with severe judgement or comments.

"To be or not to be..." the Hamlet's dilemma is a very important question which a researcher has to overcome first before selecting a research subject.

Selection of a research subject is the first step for a researcher. While selecting his/her topic the scholar should ask himself: Is it really worthwhile to pursue an enquiry in this particular field? Is it likely to contribute to knowledge in this particular area? To quote John Dewey: "It is a familiar and significant saying that problem well put in half-solved. ...To mistake the problem involved is to cause subsequent inquiry to be irrelevant. Without a problem there is blind grouping in the dark."

Next step is 'Hypothesis' followed by research design. After this a thorough review of related literature is essential. Sample design, research tools and interview schedule come next. Data collection, interpretation and analysis of data is the core of a research project. Lastly, research proposal is written and thus completes the research journey of an investigator.

Practical Approach to Research Methodology, as the name of the book sounds, we have tried here to present the research methodology in simple and coherent way. In fact, our this endeavour is an attempt to synthesise the essential information in unique blend. Clarity in perception and language leads the presentation in superb way. The basic information contained in this book is drawn from authentic sources—national and international. For clarifying different points, instances are taken from different standards works.

I am deeply beholden to all great scholars of yore days as well as present time who have paved the ways for research. In fact, entire credit goes to them all. I am grateful to my colleagues, seniors and friends for their constant inspiration and moral support. I am thankful to my father and mother for their blessings and to my wife and children for providing me a congenial work atmosphere at home. Finally, Mr. M.P. Misra, deserve all appreciation for bringing out this book in superb way.

I hope the present work will help all the researchers in their work leading to successful completion.

—SPV

CHAPTER 1

Research Problem

Derived from the Greek word "proballein" the problem means anything thrown forward; a question proposed for solution; a matter stated for examination. R.S. Woodworth defines problem as "a situation for which we have no ready and successful response by instinct or by previously acquired habit."Without a problem, research cannot proceed because there is nothing to proceed from and proceed toward.

To decide upon a suitable problem wherein researchers most valuable time, money and other energies are to invest in the process of research is the arduous task for a researcher. It is an area in which 'vision' plays an important role.

The striking and shocking aspect of higher education is its extensive passivity or intellectual non-involvement. Our system is that it is possible for a student to complete the post-graduate course and take a brilliant first class depending solely on half-a-dozen text books. It is worth to mention here that "a fresh post-graduate student is problem-blind. He has eyes but he does not see. He has ears but he does not hear." So, it is pertinent that when a student with a master's degree turns to research there is a sudden and big discontinuity in the academic process which put him excessively in oppressed state. And some time to the extent of not being able to proceed at all.

The only remedy to his problem is developing a sense of academic curiosity in collecting material and processing it; and getting conclusions putting them to tests. This sort of exercise though not full but pre-occupied can be of great help to get one's mind attuned to research. All this exercise constitute the essence of what is called `research.' The second preliminary problem is related to whether the research problem must be suggested by the supervisor or must be selected by the candidate himself.

On this issue, there are no hard and fast rules which can be laid down in general terms except that if both the supervisor and the candidate are sustained their interest in a topic acceptable to both. Neither the supervisor alone suggest a problem to the candidate nor the candidate himself welcome it. In the sense that the imposition by the supervisor and the dependency by the candidate destroy the elements of spontanity and authenticity which must mark research work.

Selecting a Research Problem

After demarcating the broad area in which one would like to do research, one must at least possess two considerations, viz. (a) interest and (b) competence. To do sustained work on a problem and to put one's intellectual efforts fully into it is a difficult task and will turn out to be a drudgery unless one has a genuine interest in the problem itself. Interest in the subject is being developed by various reasons. Example, an agricultural background student may have interest in some area related to agriculture. On the contrary, he may avoid agriculture altogether. Academic interest in a particular branch of subject may be the result of reading a good book or because of the teacher dealt with it extremely well. However, the interest of the candidate has come about and which makes sure that the area of work conforms to one's general inclinations. Interest and inclination must be matched by competence before one can decide on an area of research. *Competence* can certainly be cultivated and learning new techniques is part of any research programme.

A young researcher is often tempted to thing of himself as a potential Samuelson or Schumpter if not Adam Smith or Keynes. Such professional ambitions may be good up to a point but it is worthwhile to recall that a very few of the stalwarts in the profession have achieved fame through a doctoral dissertations. Therefore, ambition is good but too much ambition is dangerous.

On finally deciding the main area of research, the next step is to narrow it down to a topic. In fact, the supervisor can be and should be of greater assistance. A good grasp of the branch of the subject as a whole and a detailed acquitance with work already done in it are essential to suggest a topic for research. The researcher cannot be a passive recipient of suggestions but to know the field himself. This can be acquired by reading 'the literature.' After the survey of literature, the area of research problem has to be narrowed down. It means select an area on which one can get the guidance of a few competent articles or books, but not of too many. In social science research this 'rule' is utmost important. In brief, identifying a research problem is an active but subjective process, and possibly the most important aspect of research. The research is process, process of extraction and expansion; and of arriving at the end 'reforming.'

Problem of Sources

The main are sources with which one may look for a significant research problem.

1. The records of previous research, academic discussion through means of seminars, conferences, sustaining attitude towards the existing practices, are sources for a research problem.
2. The questioning attitude about existing practices and research-oriented academic experience will promote problem-awareness
3. The present educational practice is mainly learning and teaching which is still inadequate. This laid emphasis for the need and scope for performing the daily teaching by new methods.

4. The new problem and new opportunities for research have been arised because of social development and technological changes. Thus, research is born out of problem and man's determination to solve problems.

Research Problem Criteria

Many conditions and considerations have to be satisfied before finalising the problem for research. In fact, there are no standard rules that will make sure the suitability of a research problem. However, the following criteria in the form of conditions might be taken for guidance in the selection of a problem for research.

Novelty: The problem must be novel. The investigator has to find out whether enough research has been done or not before selecting the problem. Futile problems are not worth considering for research. Originality is the basic credit point of any research.

Practicability and Applicability: The original problem does ensure and have practical value to meet the society's demand. The purpose of any research should, ultimately, meet the society's problem and try to develop its economic as well as related aspects. This does not however mean that attention should not be made to solve the fundamental or pure social problems. Mere production of statistical information does not evoke, though such type of information is essential to strengthen the cause of research. Country like India should assume more attential to 'applied' research in view of its urgency as well as financial constraint of the country; and therefore cannot spend more money for 'pure' research. Therefore, the problems for research should be practicable.

Urgency: Urgency is the pinpoint in social science research. Priority must be given to the urgent problems of society because solutions of such problems immediately will benefit the people. Today, there are many urgent problems in the country. For example, the role of nationalised commercial banks in meeting the social goals, i.e. financing priority sectors on priority basis, prevention of evasion of tax, effective administration for increasing higher productivity in industrial sector, etc. The commercial banks though ventured in financing priority sectors long back but their role is limited. To know whether the commercial banks are moving in the right direction of meeting the social goals. Today many rich people evading tax and also many hoarding a lot of wealth. Unless and until, precautionary measures should be implemented for effective recovery of tax and for making black money into white money, it is difficult to meet all the social aims in the country. Similarly, for attaining self-sufficiency in production, it is our major role to increase production to which better ways and means should be innovated.

Contribution to the Subject: Research in social science is at infant stage. Although it has accredited a substantial body of knowledge, it is yet to make such progress in building scientific theories. The physical scientist often question the status of social science that it does not employ scientific methodology to find the solutions to the problems. Such type of challenge can be met only when these social scientists like physical scientists should take up scientific problem, the means thereof, will greatly add to knowledge in the field. This type of problem under research must make some addition to the development of the field of specialisation.

Anticipation: The social and economic conditions of the society are changing repeatedly due to the dynamic nature of human beings with the result so many new problems may crop up in the immediate future. So, the researcher should possess the quality of anticipation with which he may not await till the problem is born and recognised by the people.

Feasibility: The feasibility of research problem will play a greater role in selecting the problem for research. The researcher should possess the quality of carrying out the work taken up successfully with competence, knowledge and understanding, skill enough to develop, administer and interpret necessary data gathering, grounding statistical techniques. The problem should match the researcher qualification, experience and training.

Aim of Research: The aim of research also influences the selection of the problem. If it is producer research, the problem will be studied to enhance existing knowledge.

Data Availability: Data is the 'core' in research to make sure of it. Data may be of two types, viz. (a) primary and (b) secondary. The data which has no statistical analysis and collected directly from the respondents is called primary data. While the data has statistical analysis and compiled from the records and reports is known as secondary data. To make sure the research, the researcher must get data which are available readily and easily. Otherwise, it is advisable either to drop that problem or change it in a suitable manner. There are many areas in which the collection of data is difficult.

Personal Considerations of Scholar

An opportunity once lost, may be lost for ever. It is said that the qualities of researcher have equal to the problem under investigation. For instance, if problem is too wide and unmanageable, it may lead to the failure of the project. While, if the problem is too small, it may not be real challenge to the researcher which may lead into undesirable. Curiosity, objectively, discernment, sincerity, power of observation, sound and rich knowledge, scientific bent in application of advanced statistical tools, more specialist than generalist, availability of time money, and personnel, availability of administrative co-operation, and last but not least, insight are essential to recognise problem. A good researcher should always be alert and prompt.

So, it is essential to institute courses as well as seminars to purpose and inculcate the researchers the above traits. Chance favours only to prepared mind. The careful observer notices and interprets clues. The above discussion relating to the criteria for selecting a problem for research may be put in the form integrative which are as:

1. Is the problem amenable to research within the time and other resources available to researcher?
2. Is the problem sufficiency original that it does not involve objectionable duplication?
3. Are there available equipment, data, methods, sponsorship and co-operation?
4. Are the results of the research likely to be practical and utilitarian?
5. Is anticipation or expected outcome and its importance to problem of development?

Formulation of Research Problem

Needless to say, the formulation of enquiry must notice some difficulties and guide how to be removed them. In formulation of a problem for research the three principal components are to be followed. They are:

(a) Originating the question
(b) Specifying the question
(c) Rationale of question

Originating the Question: The fundamental objective of the research may specify the origin. The originating question is the first problem in the formulation of research. It discovers new and more decisive facts giving rise to the problem at hand. Some social facts explain the problem that exist but these facts may be superficial and not real. And doubt is raised about the facts themselves and hence a discovery.

Specifying the Question: The question which has originated the research must be specifically and clearly stated. A criteria may be decomposed into several specific questions, each of which can be answered separately and conveniently by the research. A particular observation becomes necessary to answer a specific question. However, every concrete situation is not *perse* strategic. It is what the investigator brings to the situation that makes it strategic. Specific questions can be precisely and successfully answered for the benefit of the society. When the answers are found to these specific questions, it is possible to find out a solution to the problem.

Rationale of Question: The rationale of question helps to distinguish between a valuable and a trivial question. The questions may be either theoretical or practical. The researcher to the questions raised may improve to theory, enlarge the scope of theory or may lead to a new theory building. The conceptualisation and understanding may be made clear by answering such questions. Thus, the questions may have either theoretical interest or practical utility. It must not neglect either of these two.

How to Proceed?

The formulation of the problem consists in making various components of the problem explicit.

Says John Dewey: "It is a familiar and significant saying that a problem well put in half-solved. To find out what the problem or problems are which a problematic situation present...is to be well along in inquiry. To mistake the problem involved is to cause subsequent inquiry to be irrelevant. Without a problem there is blind grouping in the dark."

Merton has presented a powerful case for investigating the process of problem-finding. Although the process of problem-solving has been subjected to intensive investigation, inquiries into the process of problem-finding. Merton points out, have suffered relative neglect. He makes an attempt to identify some of what is involved in seeing and formulating a problem for social research. Merton distinguishes three principal components in the progressive formulation of a problem for social research:

— The originating questions (what one wants to know?)
— The rationale (theoretical or practical) (why one wants to have the particular questions answered?)
— The specifying questions (possible answers to the originating questions in terms that satisfy the rationale).

(i) The Originating Questions: These questions represent the beginning of certain difficulties or challenges which, formulated in such specific terms so as to indicate where exactly the answers to them can be searched for, attain the status of a research problem. Thus, the originating questions constitute the initial phase in the process of problem-formulation.

One class of originating question calls for discovering a particular body of social facts. Such questions may express doubt whether the alleged social facts are really facts. Needless to say, before social facts can be explained it is advisable to ensure that they actually are facts. It is not unusual for scientists to provide explanations for things that never were. It is easy to see that, "if the facts used as a basis for reasoning are ill-established or erroneous, everything will crumble or be falsified...errors in scientific theories most often originate in errors of facts."

Another type of originating question directs attention to the search for uniformities of relations between classes of social variables. An example of such a question is "what is it in the structure of societies that determine the kinds of deviant acts that occur in various social systems."

Such questions, it would seem, are formulated in terms of broadly delimited categories of social variable but they do not indicate specifically which particular variables in each class might be germane to the issue. Such questions usually derive from a general theoretical orientation rather than a definite theory.

It should be quite evident that the originating questions differ in their scope as well as in their degree of specificity. For example, in sociology, a large number of originating questions are addressed to social variables within one or another institutional sphere of society. "Does the degree to which management takes the teacher's views into account in their decision-making affect the degree to which the teacher takes the students' views into account, in the class-room?", is one question of this type. But such relatively specific questions concerned with a particular institutional sphere (e.g., the school system) may have potential reference to comparable organizations in which role incumbents may reproduce in their behaviour *vis-a-vis* a subordinate his experience in relation to his superior.

In sum, the originating questions are of different kinds and emanate from different sources. Some are questions of descriptive fact, some put to question the adequacy of certain concepts, some are about observed empirical generalizations, some enquire into the sources of the observed patterns of social organization and others into their consequences, etc.

(ii) Rationale of Questions: The originating question is just one component of the problem. Another one is the rationale of the question. Rationale is the statement of reasons why a particular question is worth putting across. The rationale states what will happen to other parts of knowledge or practice if the question posed is answered, i.e., how the answer to the question will contribute to theory and/or practice. In this way, the rationale helps to effect a discrimination between scientifically consequentially and scientifically trivial questions. "Some problems are worth more attention than others because by their solution the conceptual structure of science is put at risk...." In short, "the rationale states the case for question in the court of scientific opinion." The requirement of a rationale curbs the flux of scientifically trivial questions and enlarge the volume of important or consequential ones.

As a rationale for science as a whole, it refers simply to knowledge as a self-contained end. It ignores, rather than denies the possibility that a new bit of knowledge will contribute to practical concerns, viz. power, comfort, safety, prestige etc. The scientist may regard his deep interest in a question and its answers are to become a part of the corpus of science, they must be shown to be relevant to other ideas and facts in the discipline. The practical rationale makes a case for the questions by pointing out that its answers will help people achieve certain practical values, i.e., health, comfort, productivity, etc. This is not to deny that a question raised mainly with an eye to the practical value of its answer may have important consequences for the theoretical system. It is evident that a particular question uses largely because the inquiry undertaken with an eye on any one, generally has unintended consequences for the other.

A question may also be considered worth asking because its answer will bridge the gaps in the existing ideas or theory that do not account for aspects of phenomena to which they should apply in principle. In some cases, the gap may be bridged by ideas that are consistent with the existing theory, which is then seen as incomplete but not wrong. In other cases, the new theoretical proposal would require some revision of earlier theory. Merton cites as illustration the question of accounting for regularities of social behaviour that are not prescribed by cultural norms or that may even be at odds with these.

(iii) Specifying Questions: This is the phase of culmination in the process of formulating a research problem. The originating questions, as we have seen, differ in their degree of specificity. Some may be quite diffuse, some relatively specific. In their most diffused form, they simply register a dimly-felt sense of ignorance, a general concern will 'something' that seems to be in need of solution but this 'something' is not clearly or sharply identified. In a somewhat

more focused form, the originating questions seem to point to a class of variables that may be involved in bringing about an observed state, without specifying the pertinent variables in that class. At this stage, the problem has yet to be fully instituted. The originating question still remains to be recast to indicate clearly the observations that will provide an answer to it.

It should be clear that not even the beginning of a solution can be found so long as the question remains in this undifferentiated or fused form. This question must, therefore, be broken down into several specifying questions related to particular aspects of organization of hospitals and their consequences for the care of patients (e.g. hierarchy of status, formal rules etc.). These simple, pointed, limited and empirically verifiable questions are then the final resultant of the phased process we designate as the formulation of a research problem. It is only such specific questions as provide answer which when synthesized afford the solution to be problem. This solution, as we have stated earlier, has implications for theory/systematic knowledge or for practice.

Necessary Conditions for Formulation of Research Problem

We may now list some of the conditions that experience has proved to be conducive to formulation of significant research problems.

(i) Systematic Immersion in the Subject-Matter through First-hand Observation: The researcher must immerse himself thoroughly in the subject-matter area within which he wishes to pose a specific problem. For example, if the researcher was interested in the general area of juvenile delinquency, it would serve him well if he visited remand homes, juvenile centres, juvenile courts, the families of the delinquents and the locality where the incidence is high. He should try to know at first hand the various aspects of the life of delinquents

by interviewing them, their family members and supervisors, etc., by observing relevant aspects about their lives. There is often no alternative to such field observation, no experience is more rewarding in terms of getting a deep feel of the situation. This exercise helps a great deal in suggesting to the researcher the specific questions that may be posed for the study to answer. This process is known by various names, e.g. pilot survey, preliminary survey or exploratory study.

(ii) Study of Relevant Literature on the Subject: We have already seen that to be able to pose a problem, the researcher must be well equipped to experience some difficulty or challenge. This in turn would depend upon the researcher being well-conversant with the relevant theories in the field, reports and records etc. This would help the researcher to know if there are certain gaps in the theories (his problem then will be to bridge these) or whether the prevailing theories applicable to the problem are inconsistent with each other or whether the findings of different studies do not follow a pattern consistent with theoretical expectations and so on. All these will afford occasions for institution of research problems. This is also an aspect of exploration.

Discussions with persons having rich practical experience in the field of study. This is often known as an experience survey, which again is an exercise at exploration. Administrators, social workers, community leaders, etc. are persons who have a rich practical experience in different fields of social life. These persons, therefore, are in a position to enlighten the researcher on different aspects of the field of his proposed study. Such persons represent in a nutshell years of experience, hence their advice, components, information and judgments are usually invaluable to the researcher. They help him sharpen his focus of attention on specific aspects within the field.

Important as these conditions are in formulating a research problem, they hide a danger. In social science as elsewhere, habits of thought may interfere with the discovery of the new or the unexpected, unless the preliminary observations, reading and discussions are conducted in a consultantly critical, curious and imaginative frame of mind.

Sources of Research Problem

The research problems may be selected from the following sources:

— Theory of one's own interest;

— Daily problems;

— Technological changes;

— Unexplored areas; and

— Discussions with supervisor.

A researcher may select a problem for investigation from a given theory in which he has considerable interest. In such situations the researcher must have thorough knowledge of that theory and should be sufficiently inquisitive to explore some unexplained aspects or assumptions of that theory. Research problem can also be selected on the basis of daily experience of a researcher. Every day problems constantly present something new and worthy of investigation and it depends on the sharpness of the researcher's intellect to knit his daily experiences into a research problem.

Technological changes in a fast changing society are constantly bringing forth new problems and new opportunities for research. What is the impact of a changed technolog on the existing socio-economic set up, always interests the researcher and tempts him to undertake such studies as are revealing regarding the impact of new technology on the existing system.

Research problems can be both abstract and of applied interest. These may also be selected from those areas which have not been explored so far; such areas may be theoretical or empirical in nature. For example, an economic analysis of hill farming systems in a region where such an investigation has not been undertaken earlier is a useful piece of research. In a similar fashion geographical regions about which no knowledge exists can easily be undertaken for research purposes.

Sometimes the researcher while discussing the interests with the proposed supervisor may come across a problem that can be researched by the investigator. The problem may relate to any source as discussed above. In the same way reading assignments in text books, special assignments, research reports and term papers may also suggest some additional areas of needed research. Many research articles suggest problems for further investigation that may prove fruitful. Such specialised sources as the *Encyclopaedia of Social Science Research, Dissertation Abstracts International* and similar other publications published by different agencies and individual publishers are rich sources for problem-seekers.

Formulating and Stating the Problem

After the problem has been selected, it must be definitely formulated and stated. If it is to serve as a guide in planning the study and interpreting its results, it is essential that the problem is stated in precise terms. The type of statement to be employed depends on the preference of the worker and the nature of the problem. Preferably it should be set as a question or in such form that the question to be answered is clearly indicated. There are two different ways of stating a problem:

— Posing question/questions.

— Making declaration statement/statements.

One may choose any of these ways remembering that the question form has an advantage in sharpening and focusing the issue, but the declarative form is perhaps more common, and both of the ways may be combined easily in an initial statement.

Definition of the Problem: It implies the separation of the problem from the complex of difficulties and needs. It means to put a fence around it, to separate it by careful distinctions from like questions found in related situations of need.

To decline a problem means to specify it in detail and with precision. Each question and subordinate question to be answered is to be specified. Sometimes it is necessary to formulate the point of view or educational theory on which the investigation is to be based. If certain assumptions are made, they are explicitly noted.

It is important to define and elucidate the problem as a whole and further define all the technical and unusual terms employed in the statement. By this the research worker removes the chance of misinterpretation of any of these crucial terms. The definition helps to establish the frame of reference with which the researcher approaches the problem.

Delimitation of the Problem: Here the investigator states the restrictions and limitations which he imposes on his study. It is statement of the limits or scope of the investigation. This statement will provide information concerning who, what, where and how many. It will determine the boundaries of the project in hand.

Again, it will be important to mention as to how many subjects will constitute the sample of the study and how they will be distributed over the institutions, geographical areas of time intervals. The age level, grade level, ability level, achievement level etc. will also have to be specified.

A recognition of the limitations of the study helps to focus attention on pertinent objectives and helps to minimise the danger of over-simplification.

A time schedule should be prepared so that the researcher may budget his time and energy effectively. Dividing the project into parts and assigning dates for the completion of each part helps to systematise the project.

Justification of the Problems

This step would prevent a wastage of research efforts on un-important or insignificant problems. Problem should be board-based enough to provide an investigation of real significance. The research worker would assess to what extent the solution of the problem would contribute for the furtherance of human knowledge. The list of the objectives of the study magnifies further its utility and importance.

Common Errors

There are a number of errors, which are committed by an average research worker, while selecting and formulating a research problem. These errors need to be carefully avoided. These are as follows:

(i) Naming a Broad Field: To choose the broad area of study instead of specific problem makes no justification; for example, to study labour problem makes no justification.

(ii) Stating it such that Investigation is Impossible: This is also common source of error in selecting and formulating the research problem.

(iii) Narrowing or Localizing a Topic: The problem may be narrowed to such an extent that it becomes too small and insignificant from research point of view.

(iv) Including in it Terms of an Unscientific, Emotional or

Biased Nature: This bias or prejudice is a constant error e.g., 'the blessings of leading profession.'

(v) Lack of Precision in the Instruments: The tool, tests or device which are proposed to be used in data collection and analysis may not be precise enough resulting in another constant error.

CHAPTER 2

Selection of the Research Subject

"To be or not to be..." the Hamlet's dilemna is a million dollar's question which an investigator has to overcome while selecting the research topic.

One of the essential qualifications that every researcher should possess is his ability to detect the possibility of pursuing a particular subject which is important and yet has not received much attention or researched. While selecting his topic the scholar should ask himself: Is it likely to contribute to knowledge in this particular area? Is it really worth-while to pursue an enquiry in this field? It is a valuable practice for a research student to job down possible topics in the course of his reading and he might later consider one of them for detailed investigation. He may also talk to those who are competent to help him. A research fellow, professor or a well-informed librarian may be of help in selecting a suitable topic. Yet another way is to go through recent journals in one's subject which often indicate the problems that are being investigated and they may contain suggestions for further investigation. Excellent examples of the type of subjects appropriate to various disciplines may be found in the compilations of doctoral dissertations issued by such agencies as *Dissertation Abstracts* or *The American Economic Review* or The United States Library of Congress.

The research guide or supervisor often suggests a problem and the research scholar starts working on it. Such a procedure, though helpful very often, may create problems for the researcher. He may find, after some time, that the subject does not interest him or is beyond the range of his understanding. He loses interest and decides to abandon it. It is, therefore, not desirable for a *research scholar to approach a faculty member for a subject of research.* And many research guides have schooled themselves as a matter of principle, not to answer questions in a form as open as this, though they are usually ready to advise on specific proposals. The true researcher is one who finds a problem for himself and tries to solve it or provide an answer to a significant question relating to a particular subject. The researcher need not think that all larger questions have been answered. This is a misapprehension. Even when books have been written on a particular problem, it will be found that still there are gaps which need to be filled. He should watch for incongruities and contradictions, points of controversy and untested conclusions. He should follow clues and suggestions obtained from reading and thinking.

In selecting a proper subject one may experience some minor difficulties at the beginning, but in the long run the more time one spends in selecting a topic the more swiftly and smoothly can one bring the entire process to a satisfactory conclusion. Besides, in many universities it is not a normally permissible to deviate from the original proposal while conducting research. In any case, a marked deviation may create problems, and it may be necessary to revise the whole scheme. In most cases minor changes occur, but such shifts of emphasis require no special permission. And this is the reason for choosing a title which is not excessively restrictive.

Though completely new and original subjects are rare, a subject that has been studied already should not ordinarily be undertaken, unless the techniques used had been faulty or the evidence produced had been inadequate or unless some new sources of information and new materials had been discovered to throw new light on the subject. Before the final selection is made the researcher will do well to ask himself whether the problem is significant or not. Of course this is a very difficult question to answer. To a person who pursues knowledge for its own sake, there is no such thing as a trivial subject. "A chain is not stronger than its weakest link and all facts fit somewhere into the great scheme of things. An apparently unimportant fact may turn out to be important in the hands of a scholar or scientist." The Researcher must be able to judge for himself whether the time, energy and expense involved in the project are justified or not. Another important consideration is the feasibility of the project. Are the necessary equipments readily available? Are there adequate library facilities? Are the techniques for testing a particular hypothesis sufficiently developed?

And this means that the researcher should beforehand acquaint himself with the resources at his disposal. Many projects require specialised and expensive equipment. Unless the researcher has a reasonable assurance that necessary equipment will be available, he should consider another topic. Library facilities are essential for research. If the scholar finds that the requisite source materials are not available, he ought to rethink about the topic he has selected. Dependence on interuniversity library loans or on the international library loan service or on xerox copies may not solve all his problems. The researcher should have access to at least the basic requirements for his work.

The subject of a dissertation, in any case, should not be decided upon hurriedly. Broad topics may be avoided, and it is important to *delimit carefully the subject of research.* Try to specify it in detail and with precision. If one chooses as one's topic 'The American Civil War' one would be almost sure to feel uneasy because nobody can possibly do justice to such a large topic. Several volumes would be necessary to cover the subject adequately. It may however, be remembered that a problem is not limited by omitting important information or leaving out essential details or presenting only part of the evidence. A problem is limited by reducing the scope of the investigation. Otherwise the topic may not be completed within the required time, and it is difficult to become an expert in a subject in two or three years. In a few cases the choice of a subject may have to be determined by keeping in view the availability of a supervisor who has the necessary expertise to conduct research in a particular area. With increasing atomisation of knowledge it may not be possible to have a supervisor with the expertise or interest in an area chosen by the researcher. In that case a scholar may have to find an institution where expert supervision may be available.

It should be remembered that it is no part of the supervisor's duty to explain how research is done. The tasks of the supervisor are not so much to inform as to give general advice and moral support. The student may believe, indeed, and perhaps for good reason, that he knows more about his topic than his supervisor. On the other hand, the scholar is less likely to know more than his supervisor about studies in general. Moreover, many supervisors are busy scholars engaged in teaching and research, and meeting him, unless for worthwhile discussions, should be put off to a later time.

Lastly, the ability of the researcher should be assessed by himself. He should ask himself the following questions: Will the topic have general applicability? Can I precisely state the purpose, scope, objectives and limitations of the study? Can I state my questions or hypotheses? Do I know the exact manner in which I will test these questions or hypotheses? Am I proficient in the technique? Am I certain that I can collect relevant data? Shall I be able to complete the work within the time limit?

CHAPTER 3
Hypothesis

Hypothesis is a proposition temporarily accepted as true in the light of what is, at the time, known about a phenomenon. It is adopted as a tool for action in the search for truth. Lundberg remarks "the gathering data with a hypothesis recognises the limitations of our senses and attempts to reduce their fallibility by limiting our field of investigation so as to avoid greater concentration of attention on particular aspects which are insignificant for our purpose." Goode and Hatt has defined hypothesis as "a proposition which can be put to test ot determine validity." Lundberg defines hypothesis as "a tentative generalisation, the validity of which remains to be tested." "In its most elementary stages, the hypothesis may be any hunch, guess, imaginative idea which becomes a basis for action or investigation." Palmer O. Johnson has beautifully described hypothesis as "islands in the uncharted seas of thought to be used as bases for consolidation and recuperation as we advance into the unknown."

Characteristics of Hypothesis

In view of the hypothesis importance and intended purposes to be served in the phenomenon of investigation, a workable or usable hypothesis must possess or satisfy the following criteria.

1. *Empirically Testable:* A hypothesis should be empirically testable. It should be framed so that it makes possible to deduce logically certain inferences which in turn can be tested. The concept embodied in the hypothesis must have empirical correspondence. For example, "good parents beget

good children" is a proposition that can qualify as a workable hypothesis.

2. *Specific:* The formulation of hypothesis should not be too vague or general. Often the researcher is persuaded to express his hypothesis so general or with grandiose a scope that it is not able to test. Stated otherwise, this temptation is suicidal. A hypothesis for which suitable and clear statement is to be developed. Therefore, specific formulation has so obvious merit of confidence leading research into practicable and significant. Specific hypothesis that is of any real use.

3. *Conceptually Clear:* The hypothesis must be conceptually clear. In other words, the concept that should be used clearly defined both in formally and operationally. The formal concept will clarify what a particular concept stands for, while the operational concept is the indicator of the concept in the field. It is noted that the concepts embodied in the hypothesis/ hypotheses be defined in a way commonly accepted and communicable. This would go a long in bringing about a cumulative growth of scientific knowledge.

4. *Related to Available Technique:* Hypothesis should be related to the available technique. In other words, after knowing the technique that has been available and applicable to measure the concepts and the variables to be incorporated, then only the hypothesis can be formulated. To quote Goode and Hatt, "The theorist who does not know what techniques are available to test his hypothesis is a poor to formulate usuable question". Therefore, a researcher must know clearly the workable technique before formulating a hypothesis. Judging the hypothesis to its researchability needs the sensible requirement of related and workable techniques. For example, to study the degree of vertical social mobility, it cannot do so because no definite technique has yet been evolved for measuring this kind of mobility.

5. *Simple:* The hypothesis should be simple and to the

point. Insight governs the essentials of simplicity. "The more insight the researcher has into the problem the simple will be his hypothesis about it". Forming hypothesis should neither more or less but is necessary to account for the phenomena.

6. *Related to the Body of Theory:* As we studied that hypothesis is formed from theory so hypothesis must be related to it. In other words, the roots of hypothesis would endow hypothesis with power of prediction which is one of the valuable attributes of good hypothesis. If the hypothesis is related to some theory, research will help to qualify, support, correct or refute the theory. The usual procedure that different scientists followed is to select small but correlated problems and their findings are consolidated and coordinated into a broader theory.

Characteristics of a Usable Hypothesis

We now turn to address ourselves to the question, "What are the characteristics of an usable hypothesis?" Let us try to answer it.

The criteria for judging the usability of the hypotheses are non else than those that help the hypotheses perform their designated functions *vis-a-vis* research and the growth of knowledge, generally. Hence a 'good' usable hypothesis is the one which satisfies may of the following criteria.

A hypothesis should be empirically testable. It should be so stated that it is possible to reduce logically certain inferences from it which in turn can be rested by observation in the field. That is, the hypotheses should have empirical referents. The concepts embodied in the hypothesis must have empirical correspondence. For example, 'Bad parents beget bad children is hardly a statement that can qualify as a usable hypothesis.'

A good hypothesis is in agreement with the observed facts. A single unexplained conflict between fact and hypothesis is disastrous to the latter. A hypothesis is entirely plausible and conceivable. It is based directly on existing data. The investigator should not omit the evidence contrary to his own opinion, should not build his argument from positive instances and neglect the negative cases, should not argue from a limited number of instances and should not make supposition from insufficient data.

A good hypothesis does not conflict with any law of nature which is known to be true. The idea involved in this principle is not very different from that expressed in the preceding principle. We know that there are a number of conflicting theories of learning and teaching. These conflicts arise partly out of the failure of research workers to produce hypotheses that are in agreement with fact, and are not in conflict with any law of nature. When we say that there can be memory tablet for strengthening memory, we are trying to disprove well established laws of nature.

A good hypothesis is expert. It is stated in a scientific and research like language and is not an ordinary statement.

It should be so designed that its test will provide an answer to the original problem which forms the primary purpose of the investigation. It should be related to available knowledge or theory concerning the original problem area.

It must be stated in final form early in the experiment before any attempt at verification is made.

The hypothesis must be conceptually clear. This point is implicit in the preceding criterion. The concepts utilized in the hypothesis should be clearly defined—not only formally but also possible, operationally, formal definition or explication of the concepts will clarify what a particular concept stands for, while the operational definition will leave no ambiguity about what would constitute the empirical evidence or indicator of the concept in the field. An ambiguous hypothesis characterised by underfined or ill-defined concepts cannot be tested since, understandably, there is no standard basis for knowing what observable facts would contribute its test. It is advisable that the concepts embodied in the hypothesis be defined in a manner commonly accepted and communicable. This would ensure continuity in researches and go a long way in bringing about a cumulative growth of scientific knowledge.

The hypotheses must be specific. Often the researchers are tempted to express their hypotheses in terms so general and with so grandiose a scope that they are simply not amenable to test. The temptation is suicidal. The researchers, therefore, would do all to avoid concepts in their hypotheses for which suitable tangible indexes have no developed. A hypothesis would include a clear statement of indexes which are to be used. For example, the concept of social class needs to be explicated in terms of indexes such as income, occupation, education, etc. Such specific formulations have the obvious advantage of assuring that research is practicable and significant. It also helps increase the validity of the results because more specific the statement or prediction, smaller the probability that it will actually be borne out as a result of mere accident or chance.

Suggestively, the hypothesis must be related to a body of theory or some theoretical orientation. This requirement concerns the theoretical rationale of a hypothesis, i.e., what will be the theoretical gains of testing the hypothesis? If the hypothesis is related to some theory, research will help to qualify, support, correct or refute the theory. A science can become cumulative only through building on the existing body of fact and theory. Will not deriving hypotheses as a rule from some theoretican base throttle ventures into new fields in which no theoretica system has developed? Will not such hypotheses lend to unnecessary repetitions? Doubts of this order may be raised by some. These objections do not have much substance since such hypotheses formulated imaginatively, besides serving the function of elaborating, extending and improving the theory, may also suggest important links between it and certain other theories. Thus, the exercise of deriving hypotheses from a body of theory may also be an occasion for a scientific leap into newer areas of knowledge. As Parsons puts it, "Theory not only formulates what we know but also tells us what we want to know."

Hypotheses should be related to available techniques. This is, of course, a sensible requirement applicable to any problem when one is judging its researchability. The researcher who does not know that techniques are available to test his hypothesis is in a poor way to formulate usable questions. In other words, the hypotheses should be formulated only after due thought has been given to the methods and techniques that can be used to measure the concepts and variables incorporated in the hypothesis.

This does not mean, however, that formulation of hypotheses which are at a given time, too complex to be handled by contemporary technique is a taboo at all times. We must not forget that if the problem is significant enough as a possible frame of reference, it may be useful whether or not it is amenable to verification or test by the techniques available at the time. The works of Marx and Durkheim have been of paramount importance to sociology even though at that time their larger ideas were not capable of being handled by available techniques. Lastly, it would be well to remember that posing of 'impossible' questions may stimulates the growth of technique. There is no doubt that some amount of impetus towards modern developments in techniques has come from criticism against significant studies which were considered inadequate because of technical limitations.

Types of Hypotheses

On the basis of level of abstraction, hypotheses may be classified under three categories:

The first type of hypotheses state some degree of uniformity among the empirical phenomena. For example, in an urban market like Kolkata, the determinants of demand for TV sets are identical for all the prominent makes, say, LG, Videocon, Samsung, etc. This is a common sense observation. The second type of hypothesis aim at testing the existence of logically-derived relationships between empirical uniformities. For example, we can compare, and then frame a sceptical proposition that there is some sort of relationship between the empirical uniformities:

(i) There exists a given magnitude of relationship between the percentage of colour TV programmes and the. demand for colour TVs in Kolkata;

(ii) The longer the time the consumers view the TV programmes, the greater the demand for TVs; and

(iii) The more the entertainment programme is in colour, the more the time the viewers spend on watching the TV etc.

The third type of hypothesis deal with a study of analytic variables between changes in one property and changes in another. The dependent variable "demand for TV" in Mumbai, Chennai and New Delhi and its relationship with the independent variables, viz. the entertainment programmes, the economic standards of the city inhabitants, the demonstration effect, the promotional budget of the company concerned, etc. are related to one another. Hence the relationship between the magnitude of change in the demand for colour TVs in these three cities for various makes, models and ranges, and the change in the independent variables can be hypothesised and tested with the help of statistical methods the co-efficient of correlation, regression models, etc.

Hypothesis Utility

Though hypothesis occupies a small space in the body of thesis or dissertation, it is as important as the research problem for investigation. Researcher cannot move without a hypothesis or two with his investigation. If he could not formulate a hypothesis, his investigation forwarded with aimless and fruitless. Mere collection of data which is likely to lead him anywhere. Thus, the hypothesis is the foundation of scientific research. If a clear, simple, specific and scientific hypothesis has been developed, it accounts for one-fourth of the research work has come to an end. The utility of hypothesis in social science research is being studied below.

1. It focusses research without it is like a random and aimless path.
2. Hypothesis acts as a guide. In other words, it is investigator's eye—a sort of guiding light in the world of research darkness.
3. It prevents blind research. It spells out the difference between precision and haphazards, between fruitful and fruitless research.
4. It provides direction to research identifying which is relevant and which is irrelevant. And prevents irrelevant review of literature and collection of useless or excess data.
5. It serves as a framework for drawing meaningful conclusions. Direct answer to the hypothesis being tested.
6. It links up related facts and information in fully understandable.

Use of Hypothesis in Different Types of Research

The use of hypothesis will vary somewhat with the type of research undertaken and the purposes to be served. In historical research the purpose may be either to produce a faithful record of the past or to extend the experiences with phenomena in the present to the past in order to make the view of the phenomena more complete. For the latter purpose, hypothetical thinking serves the conventional purposes, of limiting the research, sensitizing the observer and colligating facts. When the purpose is only to produce a faithful record of the past, little or no use is made of hypothetical thinking except in establishing the record itself.

In normative-survey research the investigator may or may not employ the hypothetical type of thinking, depending upon his purpose. If he desires merely to know the status of certain phenomena, little or no use may be made of hypothesis. If however the investigator is working with some problem for which the solution depends upon study of the status of various diversified phenomena and their relationship e.g., sex, differences in the achievement of high school pupils, hypothetical thinking may play an important role.

However, hypothesis does not appear to assume the significant role in normative-survey research that it does in either experimental or complex casual research. In these types of research, hypothetical thinking is best developed and plays an important part. Experiment is not the main source of scientific principles. It is the means of testing a deduction. Again, measurement is not the source of laws, it permits only the expression of a previously conceived law in mathematical terms.

Sources

The formulation or verification of hypothesis is a goal of scientific enquiry. A hypothesis may be developed or formulated from (a) scientific theory, (b) the findings of previous studies, (c) culture, (d) analogies, (e) personal experience, (f) pilot study, (g) Hunch, and (h) creative thinking and imagination of the researcher. Some of these are discussed vividly below.

Previous Studies: The findings of earlier research works lead in the formulation of proposition. In other words, the research based on the earlier research works may hypothesise that similar or dissimilar relationship between the variables in the present study. For example, C.H. Hanumantha Rao in his study entitled "Agricultural Production Functions, Cost and Returns in India" found that "per acre net income decreases with increase in size of holding." On the basis of this finding some scholar in his study entitled "A Comparative Study of Irrigated and Unirrigated Crops in...." noted that "per acre net income increases along with the increase in size of holding." This is a common way of the researcher who design his study with a view to replicating another study conducted in a different or similar context. Thus, the findings of one study may be formulated as hypothesis for study which aims at and puts it to test. This is because many a study in social science is exploratory in character. Thus, the hypothesis is based on the findings of other studies.

Scientific Theory: A hypothesis may stem from body of theory or scientific laws which is available to the field of research for putting it to test its validity. Generalisation is drawn from the theory itself. When it has been tested and found correct it becomes a part of the theory. In other words, a theory is known fact, logical deductions from which constitute the hypothesis which must be true if the theory is true. Thus, theory is a fertile seed-bed of hypotheses. Dubin says "hypothesis is the feature of the theoretical model closet to the things observable that the theory is trying to model." For example, "sound sleep for sound mind."

Scientific Theory: A hypothesis may stem from body of theory or scientific laws which is available to the field of research for putting it to test its validity. Generalisation is drawn from the theory itself. When it has been tested and found correct it becomes a part of the theory. In other words, a theory is known fact, logical deductions from which constitute the hypothesis which must be true if the theory is true. Thus, theory is a fertile seed-bed of hypotheses. Dubin says "hypothesis is the feature of the theoretical model closet to the things observable that the theory is trying to model." For example, "sound sleep for sound mind."

Culture: The (general) culture has a great influence upon the thinking process of human beings. In solving value-oriented problem, culture cannot lose sight of. While formulating hypothesis attention should be paid to recognise the culture of people. For example, if education habits of Indian children are taken for study, religion or moral bias, type of the family, play interest, cultural heritage of children, etc., will be studied. Another example is human happiness. Happiness has been related to income, education, occupation, social class and so on. The cultural emphasis on happiness has been productive of a very much range of hypothesis.

Analogies: Analogies are often a source of hypothesis. Reasoning is a very fertile source of hypothesis but reasoning by analogy generally is considered unacceptable as a source of proof. It is the process of ramming hypothesis from the likeness and similarity. It is assumed that the similarities between the situation is not accidental but is the result of the operation of some law common to both.

The sources of hypothesis is managerial analysis include.

A hypothesis provides the basis for investigation, and ensures, the proper direction in which the study should proceed. It facilitates the collection of adequate facts, and helps one to arrive at appropriate conclusions, suggestions and observations. In order to draw inferences, certain methods are usually employed. These are: methods of agreement, the methods of difference; joint methods; the methods of residues; and the statistical methods.

The task of deriving adequate hypotheses is essentially parallel to that of selecting suitable problems. There is no royal road to the location of a suitable problem, likewise there is no royal road to the discovery of fruitful hypotheses. The derivation of a good hypothesis demands characteristic of experience and creativity. Though hypotheses should precede the gathering of data, a good hypothesis can come only from experience. Some degree of data gathering, the review of related literature, or a pilot study must precede the development and gradual refinement of the hypothesis.

The factor of persistence is no less important. Success in an investigation depends on the considerable time and effort spent in tracing and stating tentative hypotheses.

A good investigator must have not only an alert mind capable of deriving relevant hypotheses, but also a critical mind capable of rejecting faulty hypothesis. The person who is full of ideas may be lacking in critical analysis—that is, originally may be somewhat incompatible with a critical attitude.

Importance of Hypothesis

Hypothesis has a very important place in research although it occupies a very small pace in the body of a thesis. It is almost impossible for a research worker not to have one or more hypotheses before proceeding with his work. If he is not capable of formulating a hypothesis about his problem, he may not be ready to undertake the investigation. The aimless collection of data is not likely to lead him anywhere. The importance of hypothesis can be more specifically stated as under:

— It provides direction to research. It defines what is relevant and what is irrelevant. Thus it prevents the review of irrelevant literature and the collection of useless or excess data. It not only prevents wastage in the collection of data, but also ensures the collection of the data necessary to answer the question posed in the statement of the problem.

— It sensitizes the investigator to certain aspects of situations which are relevant from the standpoint of the problem in hand. It spells the difference between precision and haphazardness, between fruitful and fruitless research.

— It is a guide to the thinking process and the process of discovery. It is the investigator's eye—a sort of guiding light in the world of darkness.

— It focusses research. Without it research would be like a random and aimless wandering.

— It prevents blind research. Prevents indiscriminate gathering of data which may later turn out to be irrelevant.

— It sensitizes the individual to facts and conditions that might otherwise be overlooked.

— It places clear and specific goals before us. These clear and specific goals provide the investigator with a basis for selecting samples and research procedures to meet these goals.

— It serves the function of linking together related facts and information and organising them into one comprehensible whole.

— It enables the investigator to understand with greater clarity his problem and its ramifications, as well as the data which beat on it. It further enables a researcher to clarify the procedures and methods to be used in solving his problem and to rule out methods which are incapable of providing the necessary data.

— It serves as a framework for drawing conclusions. It makes possible the interpretation of data in the light of tentative proposition or provisional guess. It provides the outline for setting conclusions in a meaningful way.

Different Forms of Hypothesis

The hypothesis can be stated in a number of forms which are:

(i) *Null Form:* It states that no significant difference exists between the variables concerned. For example, there is no significant difference in the instructional standards of single shift and double shift industries. The null form is preferred by most of the experienced research personnel. This form of statement more readily defines the mathematical model to be utilized in the statistical test of the hypothesis. The no-difference statement assumes that the two groups will be tested and found to be equal.

(ii) *Prediction Form:* It is chosen because it allows the research worker to state principles which he actually expects to emerge from the experiment. This type of hypothesis is more useful in action research studies.

(iii) *Declarative Form:* It generally states a relationship between the variables concerned. For example, we can state that there will be a significant difference in the instructional standards for boys and girls schools.

(iv) *Question Form:* The above mentioned hypothesis in question form may read—"Is there a significant difference in the instructional standards of boys and girls schools?"

Difficulties in the Formulation of Hypothesis

There are a number of difficulties from which a beginner may suffer at the stage of formulating a good hypothesis:

— Lack of knowledge and clarity of the theoretical framework of the area in which the investigator chooses to work.

— Lack of ability to make use of the theoretical framework logically.

— Lack of acquaintance with available research technique resulting in failure to be able to phrase the hypothesis properly.

— Vagueness of the statement: For example, a course in ethics will make a student a more ethical adult.

For ideally formulating the hypothesis for research, the

researcher has made a systematic effort. It learnt that the research problem reduces to a set of alternative means with which the investigator is in a position to pose the questions for each mean as to what would constitute the evidence for a particular mean is the most efficient one among the deternatives. Being specific conditions it is accepted as the most efficient among the alternatives. Such specific conditions are called acceptance conditions which are the hypotheses. Simply stated, the alternative hypotheses are the statements of acceptance conditions to the problem. The researcher does not know which of acceptance condition is true, this is precisely what the research is designed to determine. Thus, the formulation of hypothesis involves the steps mentioned below.

1. A measure of efficiency applicable to all the alternative courses of action is selected.
2. A set of acceptance conditions for each alternative course of action is assigned on the basis of selected measure of efficiency.
3. The acceptance conditions are reformulated as hypotheses which are mutually exclusive and jointly exhaustive.

The approach to hypotheses testing is not the constitution of a simple hypothesis about the population parameter, but rather to set up different hypothesis. These hypotheses must be constituted so that of one hypothesis is accepted or other is rejected and vice-versa. The hypotheses are normally referred to as:

(a) Null hypothesis
(b) Alternative hypothesis

A reasoing for possible rejection of proposition is called 'null hypothesis.' It is very useful tool in testing the significance of difference. H.E. Garrett remarks "the null hypothesis is akin to the logical principle that a man is innocent until he is proved guilty. It constitutes a challenge and the function of a research is to give facts a chance to refute this challenge." A null hypothesis is its other form asserts that the results found to be expected on a probability basis in terms of certain theory. As against null hypothesis, the alternative hypothesis is formulated embracing whole range of values rather than single point. For example, an alternative hypothesis may be stated that:

H_1 = The males visit cinema oftener than the females

The Null hypothesis may be stated as:

H_o = The males and females do not differ in respect of the frequency of seeing cinema

The null hypothesis is more useful than other hypothesis because it is exact. It is easier to disprove the category of the hypothesis than to prove it with certainty. According to Karl Popper, the Real basis of science is the possibility of empirical disproof. No amount of positive confirmation of a hypothesis, in Poper's view, entails its truth.

Testing Hypothesis

Any hypothesis can be subjected to test with known statistical method. The test is 'core' otherwise the research study will be incomplete. Thus, testing of an hypothesis is an essential part of the research study of the reasons that the study of statistical inference enables researcher to so much confidently examine the accuracy of (his) study results.

Data with experimental nature require to undergo a comparison of two or more relating to statistics. An evaluation of the difference between two statistics, say mean is desired. Both means are subject to error. May the difference between the two means be ascribed to sampling error or may it be due to structures differ. A decision in this regard is required between these alternatives. Statistical procedure which leads to decision of this kind is called 'Test of Significance.' It may be applied to the difference between statistics of independent samples or between statistics obtained under different conditions for the same sample. Sometimes it is applied to test the difference between a single sample statistic and a fixed value.

Fairly are two important means of testing hypothesis, viz.

(a) The study of hypothesis for 'logical consistency'

(b) The study of hypothesis for 'agreement with fact'

The study of former is a phase of thinking and gets the logical character of reasoning by hypothesis which deduces for verification as well as involved for logical consistence for agreement with known laws of nature. The suggested inferences are tested in thought, for logical consistency, before they are tested in action. In the later, one will be found, certain facts, conditions and or relations if the hypothesis is true. And it is tested with known facts for its agreement or disagreement.

An Illustration

A random sample of 18 pairs of observation from normal population gives a correlation coefficient of 0.4. Could this sample come from a population with zero correlation?

Answer

Let us take,

HO = The sample could come from a population with zero correlation

H_1 = The sample could not come from a population with zero correlation

The values given in the above problem is being studied in 't' test with n—2 degrees of freedom at five per cent. $t = r \times \sqrt{n-2} / \sqrt{1-r^2}$. The value of 't' is 1.74 and the table value is 2.12. Here the calculated value of 't' is less than the table value and therefore, the null hypothesis is true, i.e. the sample could from a population with zero correlation.

Thus, a hypothesis is never proved, it is merely sustained or rejected. If it fails to meet the test of its validity, it must be modified or rejected. The partly incorrect and negative instances which occur require only further classification and refinement of the hypothesis rather than its outright rejection.

How can the hypothesis can be verified? The answer is "By collecting data, and classifying and interpreting them." If the facts support the hypothesis, the hypothesis is true.

CHAPTER 4

Designing Research

Any social setting is a potential target for scientific examination. In spite of the diversity of possible social topics and/or situations investigated, most contemporary social scientific research is characterized by some type of study plan. This plan is conventionally labelled the *research design.*

Major Functions of Research Designs

Regardless of the *type of research* design selected by the social investigator, all plans perform one or more functions outlined and discussed below. The number of functions performed by any design largely depends upon the sophistication of it coupled with the researcher's concerns.

Without adequate drawings and plans, a homebuilder would become burdened with insurmountable problems such as where to place the foundation, what kinds and qualities of materials to use, how many workers are required, how large should the home be, and so on. By the same token, a social researcher faces comparable obstacles if he commences his study without some kind of research plan. For example he chooses to study people directly, some possible considerations might be: (1) a description of the target population about which he seeks information, (2) the sampling methods used to obtain his elements (people or things), (3) the size of sample, (4) the data collection procedures to be used to acquire the needed information, (5) possible ways of analyzing the data once collected, and (6) whether or not to use statistical tests, and if so, which one(s)? These problems are given strong consideration in a research proposal, prospectus, or study outline that many investigators elect to construct in advance of their research. An example of a research proposal will be presented in a later section of this chapter.

Without the delineation of research boundaries and/or objectives, a researcher's activities in a single project could be virtually endless. Many professors directing the work of their graduate students are probably familiar with the problem of dealing with the loose ends of an improperly planned (or unplanned) research project. With clear research objectives in view, however, investigators can proceed systematically toward the achievement of certain goals. The *structure* provided by the research plan enables the investigator to reach closure and consider any given project completed.

It is customary for researchers to review current literature central to the topic under investigation. In the course of the literature review, they may learn about new or alternative approaches to their problems. At the same time they can acquire information concerning what can reasonably be expected to occur in their own investigations. Many articles in the professional journals, as well as specialized monographs, include suggestions for further study. More important, many authors provide criticisms of their own work so that future investigations of the same or similar topics may be improved. In addition, the design can function to provide some estimate of the cost of the research, possible measurement problems, and the optimal allocation of resources such as assistants (manpower) and material.

Some Research Design Objectives

Selltiz *et al.* (1959, p. 50) indicate that research designs are closely linked to an investigator's objectives. Accordingly, they specify that research designs are *exploratory, descriptive,* and/or *experimental* in nature. Consistent with these types of research designs, they delineate four major purposes of social research: (1) to gain familiarity with a phenomenon or to gain insights, (2) to describe things, (3) to determine associations between variables, and/or (4) to test hypotheses. Few projects, if any, are conducted for purposes other than those stated above.

Regardless of the type of research design selected by the investigator or the objectives he hopes to achieve, a universal characteristic of any research plan is *flexibility*. It has been noted that a common function of research designs is to assist the investigator in providing answers to various kinds of social questions. A research plan conceived at one point in time is not necessarily free from alteration should unexpected conditions be encountered in a given social setting. The point of this brief discussion, therefore, is that research designs are guidelines for investigative activity and not necessarily hard-and-fast rules that must remain unbroken. This is an implicit assumption accompanying the treatment of all successive designs below.

Exploratory Objectives

Research designs may have predominantly exploratory objectives. Exploratory research is characterized by several features. First, it is assumed that the investigator has *little or no knowledge about the problem or situation under investigation.* General unfamiliarity with a particular group of people or other such research target does not provide the investigator with much opportunity to focus upon specific aspects of the social situation. Exploratory research has as one of its chief merits the discovery of potentially significant factors that may be assessed in greater detail and depth at a later data and with a more sophisticated type of research design.

For instance, if a researcher wanted to study social interaction patterns of inmates in prison systems but knew little or nothing about the structure and functioning of penal institutions, an exploratory research project would be in order. A preliminary investigation of several prison settings and interviews with wardens and/or other prison officials would enable the researcher to develop a more sophisticated and specific study plan.

As a second example, if an investigator wished to analyze the content of book reviews in major trade journals as a means of determining the nature and direction of interests in an academic field over a fixed time period, he would first have to determine *which* journals contained book reviews and for what years, whether there was a sufficient number of book reviews from year to year to make such a study worthwhile, whether there were stylistic differences in reviews from journal to journal examined, and what types of categorization or classification problems he would have to overcome (see Champion and Morris, 1973, for one application.) Exploratory studies, therefore, serve primarily to acquaint the researcher with the characteristics of his research target, whatever it may be.

Descriptive Objectives

Much of the sociological literature is replete with descriptive studies of all types of social situations. A few examples of the diversity of social settings as objects of descriptive studies include Andreski's (1968) portrayal of military organization and society, McCormicks's (1960) description of managerial unionism in the coal industry, Mouledous' (1963) description of the organization and goals of a prison social system, Whyte's (1948, 1949) descriptions of the social structure of the restaurant industry, Findikyan and Sells' (1966) examination of campus student organizations, Georgopoulos and Mann's (1962) study of hospital organization, Anderson's (1968) discussion of bureaucratic structure in school systems, Landy and Singer's (1961) study of the social organization and culture of a club for former mental patients, Flittie and Nelson's (1968) description of the occupational role of truck drivers, and Davis' (1959) examination of the cabdriver and his fares.

Although an exact tally of the number of predominantly descriptive studies undertaken during the past 30 years cannot be readily ascertained, it would appear from a cursory review of available literature that the bulk of sociological material in print to date is, for the most part, descriptive in nature.

Before universal patterns of social interaction can be delineated, there must be extensive descriptive material available about people under diverse social conditions. Descriptive studies provide researchers with a vast amount of information about many social settings. Describing certain characteristics of a sample or population of elements will enable the investigator to construct more sophisticated experimental research designs at a later date.

Contrasted with exploratory studies, descriptive designs are more specific in that they direct attention to particular aspects or dimensions of the research target. The heuristic value of descriptive studies must be considered a major contribution as well. Consistent with at least one of the objectives of research designs outlined by Selltiz *et al.* (1959, p. 50), descriptive studies can reveal potential relationships between variables, thus setting the stage for more elaborate investigation later.

Experimental Objectives

Designs with the objective of experimentation implicitly include the control of variables. The researcher experiments by observing the effects of one or more variables upon others under controlled conditions.

The use of the word *control* in social research has several connotations. In one sense, *control* means to *hold constant one or more factors while others are free to vary.* For instance, if the variable, sex, is believed to be a crucial factor in an experimental situation, sex is controlled by observing the differential reactions of males in contrast with females to a specific stimulus or experimental variable. An experimental variable may be a sound, an electrical shock administered to the skin, a dosage of drug, a social situation, or any other external condition to which the sample of males and females is exposed. If we control for the variable, age, this variable is said to be held constant. In other words, how do all individuals between the ages sixteen to nineteen behave compared with individuals in the age category twenty to twenty-three when exposed to a common stimulus?

A hypothetical sample of college students and a distributional arrangement of their attitudes (favourable or unfavourable) toward premarital sex. This table gives us some general information about what this sample of students thinks about premarital sex. If we wish to control for sex, we would differentiate the students into sex *subclasses*, male and female. The students' attitudes toward premarital sex, but in this instance we have *controlled for sex.* A much more specific appraisal of the impact of the variable, sex, on attitudes toward premarital sex. We may even find year in school as a control to be advantageous as well. Of course, if we wanted to control for both sex and year in school, our table would be somewhat more complex and would appear similar. If our sample were sufficiently large, we could legitimately derive the percentage of the actual frequency distributions throughout all cells shown in the table and determine several things about attitudinal differences of individuals compared by year in school and sex. It should be noted that continuing the addition of control variables and subdividing the table will decrease substantially the cell frequencies. For statistical analysis purposes, this makes the job of interpreting what we find increasingly difficult. The decreasing of cell frequencies not only makes it less legitimate to derive the percentage of the data we have, but for statistical and/or theoretical reasons beyond the scope of this text, any extensive data analysis becomes increasingly meaningless.

In another sense, the word *control* is used to refer to a group or an individual not exposed to *an experimental variable.* For instance, if we were to administer a drug to one group of persons and withhold the drug from another group, the group receiving the drug would be called the experimental group, whereas the other group (not receiving the drug) would be called the control group. Sometimes each individual acts as his own control. This is usually in a before/after experimental situation. A person or persons receive a stimulus (experimental variable) in one time period, and some behaviour they exhibit is measured. Then in a second time period (the time interval between the first and second time periods varies widely according to the researcher's interests and the type of experiment conducted), the same behavior is noted that was observed in the first time period. The two behaviors for the same individual or group are compared to determine the effect or effects of the experimental variable. *The individual or group is said to act as (his) (their) own control(s).*

Research designs, therefore, may have exploratory, descriptive, or experimental objectives. Many research designs include elements of all three types. There is some exploration associated with description. There is some description associated with experimentation, and so on. Implicit in this discussion is that various research projects *emphasize* specific objectives but may include others by way of secondary considerations.

Some Conventional Research Design Types

In this section we will examine several conventional research designs used by social scientists to answer various kinds of questions. Perhaps the two most popular research designs chosen by sociologists and affiliates of their profession are (1) the survey and (2) the case study. A third type of research design that assumes numerous forms is labelled experimental. Special attention will be directed toward several popular experimental research designs in a later portion of the present discussion.

The Survey Design

Survey research has been defined simply as "gathering information about a large number of people by interviewing a few of them" (Backstrom and Hursh, 1963, p. 3). Hyman (1955) differentiates between descriptive and explanatory surveys, and although no formal definition of a survey design is apparent in his work, there does seem to be implicit in

Hyman's work a general consistency in the meaning of survey research with that provided by Backstrom and Hursh (1963, p. 3).

It should be noted that a survey design may serve many functions including exploration, description, and experimentation. The general nature of a survey design is subject to little variation, however. We would seek to modify the definition of Backstrom and Hursh by defining survey designs as specifications of procedures for gathering information about a large number of people by collecting information from a few of them. There are several data collection alternatives available to the survey researcher in addition to interviewing (e.g. questionnaire administrative, personal observations, and the like).

Regardless of the objectives sought by the individual survey researcher, there are several standards to which he would like to adhere. These focus primarily on the quality of the survey. The quality of a given survey, in turn, depends on (1) the number of people one is able to obtain for the study, (2) their typicalness in relation to the population from which they are selected, and (3) the reliability of the data collected from them. The first two criteria of survey quality are directly related to the problem of *sampling*. Sampling means to select a few people from a larger collection of them. Since the researcher is most likely interested in generalizing the findings obtained from his sample to the population from which they were drawn, it is necessary that he select his sample of persons according to certain rules of probability theory.

The third criterion of survey quality—the reliability of data—is dependent on the extent to which the researcher obtains the cooperation of persons he studies. If he asks them questions (such as in an interview situation), he wants them to tell the truth about whatever they are asked. Because there is no way of forcing people to tell the truth, the researcher must often relegate this dimension to the philosophical level.

In essence, this means that the investigator accepts the information obtained from a survey subject to all of the potential limitations on it.

One example of survey research is a study of social class, parental encouragement, and educational aspirations by Sewell and Shah (1968, pp. 562-63). They selected at random 10,318 Wisconsin 1967 high school seniors (about a third of the total number of high school seniors for Wisconsin that year). "Information was obtained from the respondents, school authorities, and a statewide testing program on a number of matters, including the student's educational and occupational plans, the student's percentile rank in measured intelligence, the socioeconomic status of his family, his rank in his high school class, his course of study, and the educational attitudes of the student and his family." The primary purpose of the study by Sewell and Shah was to examine the relationship between socioeconomic status and college plans. The basic conclusion of their study (reflecting the explanatory nature of it as well as its descriptive aspects) was that

> ...the correlational, causal, and cross-tabular analyses of this study substantiate, on the whole, the claim made by other investigators using less rigorous methods and less representative samples that parental encouragement is a powerful intervening variable between socioeconomic class background and intelligence of the child and his educational aspirations. While parental encouragement does not "explain" social class differences in aspirations, it contributes to the explanation of these difference (Sewell and Shah, p. 571).

Another example of survey research is a study of maternal employment and anxiety over the mother role by White (1972). In the spring of 1965, a sample of women sixteen years of age or older was mailed a questionnaire containing items about employment status, age, number of children, care provided for small children during mother's absences, and so on. Of the 15,000 population (a small community in south-central Washington), 1,092 questionnaires were returned completed.

In this survey, several hypotheses were tested relating to anxiety over the mother's role between employed and nonemployed mothers. On the basis of the information obtained (responses to the questionnaires), it was tentatively concluded that, as a concept, status conflict appears to be useful in the prediction of certain kinds of anxiety. Some of the hypotheses concerning middle-class and working-class mothers were not upheld, however. Therefore, the study suggested potential weaknesses in traditional notions sociologists have about the implications of particular kinds of child-rearing philosophies.

Both of these studies as examples of survey research involved contacting a sample of individuals from a larger population. On the basis of information obtained (either through questionnaire, interview, direct observation, or combinations of these data collection techniques), certain assumptions and hypotheses were subjected to test, several dimensions of group behavior were more extensively described, and several insights were achieved regarding the respective problems under investigation.

Some Major Advantages of Survey Designs

1. *The most apparent advantage of survey designs is the accumulation of information from individuals at relatively low cost to the researcher.* Surveys, particularly those involving the use of mailed questionnaires, are an inexpensive means of obtaining information from large numbers of people without contacting them directly. If interviewing is used, the costs of research soar drastically. Researchers must train persons to develop appropriate interviewing techniques and skills. Little time usually exists for such preparation. If professional interviewers are used from some research agency, potential costs per interview could run as high as $ 30 or more.

2. *Because large numbers of persons are usually included in a survey, generalisability to larger populations is more legitimate.* Public opinion polls of presidential elections are frequently of the survey type. Trends about population behaviors are

inferred on the basis of the attitudes of the select number of individuals drawn from the larger human aggregate. One is cautioned, however, to scrutinize carefully the representativeness and/or typicalness of the sample obtained in relationship to the characteristics of the population about which inferences will be made.

3. *Flexible Surveys to permit the use of a variety of data collection techniques.* Observation, interviewing, and/or questionnaires can be used in survey designs to collect information from individuals. Which of the techniques will be used is a decision the researcher(s) have to make.

4. *Surveys sensitize the researcher to potential problems that were originally unanticipated.* Surveys requesting written responses and/or verbal reactions from respondents often uncover facts previously unknown to the investigator. In this sense, surveys perform an exploratory function, and serendipitous findings should not be entirely unexpected.

5. *Surveys are useful tools that enable investigators to verify theories.* The survey is one way of obtaining support or lack of support for particular theoretical notions about people.

Some General Disadvantages of Survey Designs

1. *Surveys are superficial reflections of population sentiments.* Seldom can researchers take the time to obtain in-depth information about the personal opinions and attitudes expressed by respondents, especially when questionnaires are used.

2. *Surveys, particularly political surveys, are unstable reflections of population characteristics.* Attitudes toward busing school children, increasing or decreasing federal aid to education, and the like are apt to elicit strong reactions from prospective respondents. The major problem centers on the fluctuation of opinion about such matters, however. A survey of opinions of a sample of individuals one week may be quite different from a similar survey of the same individuals a week or two

later. Speeches by political leaders, international and national affairs, management and union clashes, stock market trends, and campus discontent and disruption among other things can bring about drastic changes of opinion of a given sample of individuals. One type of survey design, *the panel design,* is indicative of attitudinal instability of a given segment of individuals.

Panel designs are useful for revealing trends and are especially applicable during political campaigns. A cross section or representative sample of individuals from a larger population of elements. These individuals are examined in five successive time periods regarding their attitudes toward a particular issue or political candidate. The fluctuations observed from one time period (t_1) to the next (t_2) are usually attributable to some intervening phenomenon (a speech, political decision, or some other significant political or social action). Forecasts of outcomes of elections are based on trends observed from panels of persons observed over time.

3. The researcher has little or no control over individual responses to surveys. Those responding differ from those who do not respond on at least one dimension—response vs. nonresponse. The potential bias resulting from such surveys (which is difficult, if not impossible, to determine) significantly limits the generalisability of one's findings to total populations from which the original samples were obtained (Clausen, 1969).

4. Statements about populations from which samples are obtained are tentative. Response is indicative of potential interest in the topic being investigated or the information requested. The researcher manipulates the data obtained by tabular and statistical analyses and arrives at tentative conclusions relative to some nation help (in some instances) about the target population. This is not really a serious disadvantage, inasmuch as social scientists (as well as *all* scientists) are obligated by their respective professional codes and orientations to regard their research findings with caution and to take into account the potential limitations accompanying research projects from start to conclusion.

The Case Study Design

Although some researchers argue that case studies do not qualify as "design" (e.g., Hagedorn and Lobovitz, 1971, pp. 36-41 designate research designs in general as "the logical manner in which individuals are compared and analyzed"), case studies constitute one of the most popular types of research designs used by social scientists currently (in the context of the definition below). Foreman (1948, pp. 408-9) provides one of the clearest definitions of a case study and situations to which the definition may pertain. He says

"....a case study, basically, is a depiction either of a phase or the totality of relevant experience of some selected datum. When the investigator's attention is focused on development, the account is a case history. When a panoramic view of the present is obtained, case studies may be called cross-sectional or photographic. In either instance the datum may in sociological study be any of the following, taken singly or in combination: (1) a person, (2) a group of persons such as gang or family, (3) a class of persons such as professors or thieves, (4) an ecological unit such as a neighborhood or community, (5) a cultural unit such as a fashion or institution."

He goes on to note that "case study materials may come to the social scientist by way of (a) personal documents, (b) participant observation records, or (c) third person reports." These are discussed as various means of data collection in the chapters noted. Extensive discussions of their limitations and strengths accompany their definition and elaboration.

Because so many subareas of sociology exist presently, it is difficult, if not impossible, to provide the reader with an example of a "typical" case study design. One example from the formal organizational literature is the work of Champion and Dager (1967), who conducted a case study of a bank undergoing changes as the result of the introduction of an electronic data processing (EDP) computer system. According to the authors, virtually every important facet of bank activity including employee sentiments was scrutinized carefully before, during, and after the changeover to EDP. Such data collection procedures as interviewing with tape-recorders, personal observation, and questionnaire administration were used to obtain information about the nature and consequences of the change process. Background characteristics of each employee were compiled that included among other things crude approximations of personality profiles. Champion and Dager not only described the changeover to EDP in considerable detail, but they also developed a tentative distinction between those employees who appeared to adapt successfully to the changeover and those who were not adaptable to the change. *The fact that the research constituted a case study did not alter the tentative nature of the interpretation of findings.*

Although definitional variations exist among social scientists regarding case studies, most would tend to agree that primary distinctions between case studied and surveys would be the *intensity* and *depth* of the investigation. Case studied are usually characterized as thorough examinations of specific social setting or particular aspects of social settings, including in varying detail psychological descriptions of persons in those settings.

A series of case studies was conducted during the mid-1950s by the U.S. Department of Labor Bureau of Labor Statistics. These pertained respectively to a modernized petroleum refinery, an automatic airline reservation system, and several insurance companies. Some additional examples of case studies may be found in the work of Chinoy (1955) who studied intensively 62 automobile workers in a large factory through interviewing and participant observation; the classic investigation of the structure and process of a community, "Middletown," by the Lynds (1929, 1937); Sayles' (1958, p. 6) in-depth descriptions of workmen in hammershops, shipping departments, metal disking, and punch press departments derived from "an examination of work records, interviews, and observations of 300 work groups in thirty plants in a variety of industries"; and Argyris (1958) case study of a bank.

Some Major Advantages of Case Study Designs

1. *Case studies are flexible with respect to data collection methods used.* Interviews, observation, questionnaires, and other data collection forms are possibilities for use in-depth analyses of specific social situations.

2. *The flexibility of a case study extends to virtually and dimension of the topic studies.* Although a chief characteristic of case study designs is thoroughness of the investigation, specific aspects of the individual or social situation studied are emphasized while other aspects are not included. This mean that although we may do a case study of a bank, for example, we focus on all important dimensions of bank activity that are important to us from the theoretical perspective we have developed. Needless to say, there are additional bank characteristics that do not logically fit into our data collection scheme. Although the Lynds (1929) studied "Middletown" in considerable detail, it is expected that certain dimensions of community life escaped their careful scrutiny. These were probably due to intentional exclusions because the particular dimension(s) in question did not fall within their theoretical and/or substantive concerns. By the same token, some dimensions were not investigated because the Lynds may have been unaware of the existence of them and/or their theoretical relevance to the purpose(s) of their study.

3. *Case studies may be conducted in practically any kind of social setting.* The primary factors affecting the selection of specific research sites are (a) the accessibility of elements, (b) the costs of the research, and (c) the time and manpower restrictions within which the researcher must operate.

4. Case studies offer specific instances of tests of theories. Provided that the investigator has adequately prepared a theoretical framework within which to cast his research activity, a case study may provide him with an opportunity to put one or more aspects of the theory to empirical test. As was indicated, theory verification may be approached from several alternative perspectives. A case study may be viewed as a test of a more general theory to the degree that a survey design is able to achieve the same objective. Both types of research designs have their respective limitations and strengths regarding generalisability, however. A survey makes possible certain generalizations to the extent that the elements surveyed are representative of the population from which they are drawn. Similarly, a case study design has as its major concern typicalness for purposes of generalisability. An intensive case study may be equally generalisable to larger social situations or aggregates compared to the more superficial survey.

5. Case studies may be quite inexpensive, depending upon the extent of inquiry involved and type of data collection technique(s) used. Certainly a researcher's costs are kept to a minimum where data can be collected first-hand and in-depth from on-the-job experiences. It is not unusual to find researchers conducting case studies of social settings of which they are a part. This stems from the fact that their affiliation with the organization or group studied supports and helps to legitimize their research efforts. They are not outsiders and do not encounter refusals as often as outsiders.

Some Major Disadvantages of Case Study Designs

1. Perhaps the most prominent disadvantage of case studies is their limited generalisability. Although case studies are conducted in such a way as to provide detailed information about social units, they are often criticized as being limited in scope and not sufficient for meaningful generalizations to be made to larger social aggregates. Again, we encounter the problem of the representativeness of the case. Of course, representativeness is a primary question in the assessment of the quality and generalisability of surveys as well.

On the theoretical level, however, it may be argued that findings from case studies lend support to or provide refutation of theories. The researcher does not regard case study findings as conclusive proof of anything. Neither does the survey researcher. Only through the accumulation of findings from many case studies and many surveys investigating similar phenomena can we begin to generate statements about the social world that have little or no exception.

2. *Case studies are generally more time-consuming contrasted with surveys.* Case studies frequently involve the direct participation of the researcher in the recording and collection of salient information. Some survey designs can be equally time-consuming, however, particularly those in which personal interviews are utilized as the primary mode of data collection.

A Concluding Note on Surveys and Case Studies

A survey derives elements from a total population. Characteristics of the sample of elements are generalized tentatively to the entire population of elements.A case study in relation to an "unknown" population. The typicalness of a case study in relation to some population is all but impossible to assess. However, because a social situation is involved, certain theoretical propositions and hypotheses can be put to test, again on a tentative basis.

It should be clear that both types of research designs discussed above may be used to test hypotheses. In fact, in some instances, both designs can be used to test the *same hypotheses.* Case studies appear to have greater utility for hypothesis tests about the structural and procedural characteristics (e.g., mobility patterns, status relations, interpersonal characteristics) of specific social units (e.g., organizations, small groups, cliques, communities). In addition to their descriptive value, surveys are of great utility for testing hypotheses about large social aggregates (e.g., female voters between twenty-one and thirty-five, Republican attitudes toward certain community issues, prejudicial reactions of specific target groups toward certain ethnic and/or racial minorities).

Experimental Designs

This final section on research designs is about a very large number of strategies geared to assess the effects of particular variables on people under heavily controlled conditions. All such designs that seek to control conditions within which persons are observed and analyzed may be called *experimental designs*. The totality of experimental designs in social research runs the gamut from very simple to extremely complex. Several books exist that include extensive descriptions of many kinds of experimental designs.

Before commencing our discussion of various kinds of experimental designs, it will be helpful to treat briefly the subject of *control groups*. The word *control* was touched on in an earlier section of this chapter in relation to studies with experimental objectives. By way of review, a control group is defined as one that is either (1) not exposed to an experimental variable and compared with a group which is exposed to it, or (2) used as the target of research by being observed prior to an experimental variable, exposed to the experimental variable, and then observed after exposure to the experimental variable. In other words, the single control group acts as its own control.

Control groups are used in experimental designs so that the researcher may ascertain the effect(s) of an experimental variable or variables on an experimental group or groups. Reviewing again, an experimental group is one that is exposed to an experimental variable. Therefore, a control group and an experimental group can be the same group when the individuals in the group act as their own controls in response to the experimental variable over *k* time periods. Variations in the uses of control groups.

The major problem related to the use of control groups with independent experimental groups is the degree of their similarity. Obviously, an experiment with a particular drug using a control group composed exclusively of women and an experimental group composed entirely of men will demonstrate little or nothing. If a difference in the behavior of men exposed to the experimental variable is observed where no change is observed in the control group composed of women, very little, if anything, can be said about the effects of the drug on the experimental group in relation to the control group because the two groups differ so dramatically regarding sex composition. This is to say that the drug may have an effect on men, but it may not affect the women. In fact, the drug may have no effect at all if the change in the behavior of the experimental group is owing to chance (which is always a possibility) regardless of whether or not the groups are similar or different.

Researchers, therefore, attempt to equate experimental groups with control groups on as many salient characteristics or dimensions as possible (e.g., age, rural or urban background, socioeconomic status, sex, years of education, and the like). Then, when changes do occur within the experimental group but not within the control group, the investigator is on firmer ground for tentatively inferring that a cause-effect relation between the experimental variable and the observed behavior change exists, and furthermore, that such changes are not likely owing to significant differences between the experimental and the control groups in terms of their most salient characteristics.

Apart from using each individual as his own control, there are at least three popular methods for achieving control group-experimental group similarities. These are: (1) individual matching, (2) random assignment, and (3) group distribution matching.

Individual Matching

Judged by many social scientists to be the most difficult method of equating groups, individual matching involves matching each individual in the experimental group with a person with very similar characteristics as a member of the control group. Considering the infinite number of personality variables that exist in addition to such factors as age, sex, years of education, occupation, I.Q., and so on, the task of individual matching becomes almost insurmountable. The result of such a matching method is usually to end up with extremely small samples of elements as experimental and control groups because so few people can be matched according to an extended list of salient characteristics. This is where using each individual as his own control becomes functional. This method overcomes problems of having to take into account random factors over which the researcher has little or no control (or knowledge), because each person is presumed to be the *same person* throughout successive time periods with the exception of changes in behaviors that are the targets of experimental variables.

Random Assignment

Random assignment as a means of equating groups is somewhat poor. This is because the researcher has no former or present knowledge of the salient characteristics of the randomized group members. Such a method would be comparable to taking a university faculty of size N (let's use the number, 200), and randomly assigning or placing each faculty member in an experimental group or in a control group. Supposedly, the randomization of assigning faculty to each group mixes the groups substantially and overcomes any bias on the part of the researcher regarding group assignment. In reality, the true characteristics of both groups are not fully known (and may not even be partially known), and it is extremely difficult, if not impossible, to say with any degree of assurance that both groups have been properly equated.

The same problem is encountered by a researcher who would take an introductory sociology class (N=100) and randomly distribute class members into two groups, one experimental and the other control. Labeling one group experimental and the other group control gives us no confidence that the groups are truely equated on any significant dimensions. The fact is there may be so much variation in student characteristics throughout the class that the researcher will not be able to know with any degree of assurance whether the difference(s) in behavior, if any, among the experimental group as a result of some experimental variable(s) are attributable to the group composition or to the experimental variable. What if the control group target behavior changes but the experimental group target behavior does not?

Group Distribution Matching

An improvement over both of the above methods, group distribution matching involves selecting certain characteristics such as age, education, I.Q., socioeconomic status, sex, specific attitudinal similarities, and the like and locating two groups that have these characteristics distributed similarly throughout. In other words, two groups may be found that are of the same age pattern, socioeconomic pattern, I.Q. distribution, sex distribution, and attitudinal position. Selltiz *et al.* (1959, p. 107) caution that "although distributions on single factors are equated, the groups may actually be badly mismatched on combinations of these factors." Extending this caution to the present discussion, the same phenomenon could possibly occur, even if we successfully were to match two or more groups on several characteristics. They could be mismatched on variables that are theoretically and/or substantively relevant but which have been excluded intentionally or unintentionally.

Using Each Individual as His Own Control

Where matching of any kind is not a consideration, observations are normally taken on a group in a preexposureto-the-experimental-variable-time-period. Then, the group is introduced to the experimental variable. Finally, observations of the group are made after the experimental variable has been introduced. Changes in specified behaviors (targets of the experimental variable) are assumed to be attributable to the experimental variable rather than to random differences on the part of the individuals participating in the experiment.

There are cautions associated with this type of plan as well. If a time interval of sufficient length occurs between each observation, any observed changes in behavior among group members may be due to extraneous factors not immediately apparent to the investigator. The maturation of the subjects, possible changes in their jobs or family lives and the like, can create false impressions of true effects of the experimental variables. The researcher must, therefore, regulate carefully the time interval between observations and do all within his power to ascertain whether or not any factors not considered initially could have intervened between observation periods to bring about the target behavior change.

Although much more space could be devoted to the advantages and disadvantages accompanying each of the methods of control discussed above, we will now move on to treatments of several conventional social scientific experimental designs.

Three major experimental designs will be discussed here: (1) the classical experimental design, (2) the after-only experimental design, and (3) the before-after experimental design.

The Classical Experimental Design

Goode and Hatt (1952, pp. 76-78) offer a verbal as well as a diagrammatic description of the classical experimental design. They define it by making reference to one of John Stuart Mill's methods of proof, namely, the method of difference. Goode and Hatt state that

> ... in its simple statement, it can be formulated in this fashion: If there are two or more cases, and in one of them observation Z can be made, while in the other it cannot; and if factor C occurs when observation Z is made, and does not occur when observation Z is not made; then it can be asserted that there is a causal relationship between C and Z.

The classical experimental design may be illustrated by hypothetical sociological example. Suppose we were to obtain two samples of individuals matched on several social and psychological variables with the exception that in one group, all subjects would have a master's degree or higher level of education while the numbers of the other group would possess only the bachelor's degree. Suppose further that we wished to obtain responses from both group concerning same community political issue (e.g., zoning restrictions governing the location of liquor stores, fluoridation of the city water supply, or the like). If the outcome of our investigation revealed that 90 per cent of the more highly educated group responded favorably to the proposed changes in the community (regarding any issue, for the matter), and that 85 per cent of the less educated group responded unfavorably to the some proposals, it would appear that the educational differential between the two groups was contributory toward (if not the direct cause of) the attitudinal differences clearly observed.

Goode and Hatt (1952, pp. 78-81) are careful to point out some of the major weaknesses of such a design, especially when it comes to establishing the "proof" of the experiment. They include (1) an inability to control relevant variables in the research project, (2) lack of clarity in the causal relation between the two variables, (3) the unpredictable effect of the time factor, and (4) the oversimplification of cause-effect relations as major weakness of this design.

After-Only Designs

Many experimental designs intended as improvements

on the classical design are, for the most part, only modifications of it (Goode and Hatt, 1952, p. 81). The after-only design seeks to compare an experimental group with a control group *after* an experimental variable has been introduced to one group and not to the other. For example, assume that two hypothetical work crews have been matched according to several important characteristics. Both groups have supervisors who allow the men much latitude in determining their own method of job performance. Assume further that in one group, the experimental group for our purposes, a change in supervisor occurs. The new supervisor over the experimental group is authoritarian and does not permit much latitude regarding job performance. Job satisfaction measures for both groups are obtained and scores tabulated and compared.

With these figures we might assume that the supervisory change led to low job satisfaction among the experimental group members. This may or may not be true. What were the job satisfaction scores of the workers before the change in supervisors was introduced ? Are other possible factors operating in the "after" situation that would affect the changes in scores (e.g., a raise in pay for one group while the other group receives no raise, changes in working hours or work shifts between the two groups, and so on) ?

These kinds of questions identify some of the major weaknesses of the after-only experimental design. The impact of the experimental variable on the experimental group is assessed in relation to the dis-parities in *scores between both groups*. The importance of after-only study designs depends in large part on the extent to which the two groups (experimental and control) are similar in social and personal characteristics. Because no matching method discussed above is infallible or perfectly effective at achieving precise matches between experimental and control groups, and because little or nothing is known about attitudinal dispositions of respective group members before obtaining measures of the target variable(s), after-only experiments should be viewed with much caution. This is especially critical when it comes to drawing tentative conclusions about causal relations between two or more variables.

The Before-After Design

The before-after design is a considerable improvement over the after-only design. Basically, the before-after experimental design consists of obtaining measures on some target variable or variables for at least two groups that are assumed to be matched according to certain previously specified criteria. The experimental variable is introduced to the experimental group and withheld from the control group. Measures are again taken for both groups on the target variables. This enables researchers to argue more effectively about causal relations between experimental variables and target variable changes, because the measures for both groups are compared between two separate time periods. It is assumed that the experimental group will be affected predictably by the experimental variable and that this will be revealed by comparing both the experimental and the control group scores on the previously designated target dimensions.

The control groups members observed in both time periods are not exposed to the experimental variable and are expected to reflect scores similar to those they revealed in the original time period.

The principal advantage of the before-after experimental design is the ability of the researcher to evaluate experimental and control group subjects both before and after experimentation and to isolate and eliminate (or take into account, take into consideration) extraneous factors that might otherwise obscure the true effect(s) of the experimental variable. The before-after experimental design using an experimental and a control group. As usual, the problem of matching individuals in the experimental situation becomes a difficult task and opens to criticism the findings based on experimental group-control group comparisons.

There are many other varieties of experimental designs utilizing different numbers of control groups and randomizing the introduction of experimental variables where *k* time periods are involved. It is beyond the scope of this book to cover such extensions of the before-after method identified above. The reader is advised to consult specialized sources, particularly Winer (1971), for more elaborate experimental designs if needed.

The concluding two sections of this chapter will discuss in some detail the preliminary elements in the research process—research proposals and pilot studies.

A Basic Outline for a Research Proposal

Ideally, all social research is preceded by a research proposal. A research proposal is a relatively brief statement of the problem to be investigated. It also includes specific study objectives, a representative review of literature pertinent to the problem, a theoretical and/or substantive justification for the study, and some methodological guidelines.

The research proposal is refereed to by different names according to the type of research it precedes. For instance, a doctoral student preparing for a doctoral dissertation may refer to the research proposal as a dissertation proposal. A master's candidate may prepare a thesis prospectus. Others may simply refer to the proposal as research plan, although as we have indicated, the notion of research plan is frequently used synonymously with research design. In order to avoid possible semantic problems, research plans may be viewed as integral components of the proposal or prospectus. Research plans constitute the methodological portion of the proposal.

Research proposals vary in length, complexity, and/or sophistication according to the particular standards of the investigator(s) in charge of the research activity. The format of a research proposal presented below is by no means to be considered the only way of outlining a project for social investigation. The various components included (as well as the order in which each is presented) are merely suggested as constituting a possible compilation and arrangement of the bare essentials. Many departures from the scheme below are to expected, especially when we consider the vast array of topics of social interest as well as the diversity of researcher preferences that exists.

One way of outlining a research proposal is as follow:

1. Introduction.
2. Statement of objectives.
3. Review of the literature.
4. Theoretical structure and/or conceptual scheme.
5. Hypotheses.
6. Methodology.
7. Statement of theoretical and substantive implications.

Short discussions of each of these components are provided below. The discussion are general in nature. They are included to indicate the importance and/or significance of each section, and they are designed to be broadly applicable to projects reflecting diverse interests.

Introduction

The introduction of a research proposal should place the problem to be studied in some kind of historical perspective. The researcher should briefly illustrate the historical development of the current problem under investigation. He should also locate his particular interests in the problem fairly precisely. In short, the researcher reveals the problem to be studied and what dimension or dimensions of it will be given extensive analysis or treatment. For example, if a researcher were to be interested in studying the social and psychological effects of automation in the business setting, he might begin by describing the early origins and applications of automation in various work environments. He could follow up this historical description by discussing present uses of automation in specific settings. At this point, he could reveal his precise interests in learning about the potential social and psychological impacts of automation in contemporary businesses.

Statement of Objectives

The objectives of research projects detail what the researcher wishes to accomplish as a result of his investigative activity. What are the specific goals to be achieved? Sometimes this section is broken down into subparts to include major and minor objectives. There are primary concerns of the investigator as well as secondary ones. In this event the researcher possibly arranges his objectives in a hierarchical fashion, listing them from most important to least important. Some proposals make explicit the distinction between major and minor (primary and secondary) objectives (goals).

There is no limit to the number of research objectives. Decisions as to how many objectives will be identified are based on the breadth of the research, the interests of the investigator, time, cost, and manpower considerations. Some studies may have a single objective whereas other projects may have twenty or thirty of them. Although there are no limitations concerning the number of research objectives a project may have, it is possible for the investigator to bite off too much of a given problem. There is little wisdom in spreading oneself too thin, however. If a researcher has too many research objectives, he may encounter great difficult in trying to tie together a lot of loose ends. Too many research objectives also necessitate a more complex theoretical scheme. Therefore, it is recommended that the investigator limit his objectives to a reasonable number. What is "reasonable" again depends on the time limitations, budgetary considerations, and manpower restrictions under which the researcher must work.

Fairly precise statements of objectives are functional guidelines for research activity. Using the automation example cited above, vague or nebulous objectives might be "to see if the introduction of automation into an employee work setting will bring about attitudinal change" or "to see if the introduction of automation will bring about significant role changes among employees." These statements are considered vague because they fail to specify which attitudes which employee roles are involved and affected by automation. Of course, it can be argued that an exploratory study may be loosely constructed so as to identify more specific research targets to be investigated with greater precision at a later date. But it would be more meaningful to state which attitudes of employees are considered most relevant for examination. A more specific statement of an objective might be "to investigate the impact of the introduction of electronic data processing [a form of automation] on employee depersonalization [an attitudinal variable]." This statement clearly indicates that the independent variable, automation, may be followed by a change on a specific dependent variable, depersonalization. One interest of the researcher, therefore, is to examine the relationship between these variables as a means of more accurately depicting potential implications of technological change on people in work environments.

Review of the Literature

The literature review is designed to familiarize the investigator with any relevant information pertaining to the topic being studied. Opinions vary concerning the extent to which a literature review should be conducted. Some researchers may be concerned with identifying all available literature on a given subject, whereas others are content to review literature in major professional journals for the most recent 10 years period. In a research proposal it is usually not necessary to discuss all literature uncovered by the researcher. A positive feature of a proposal literature review is to highlight representative ideas from articles and books on the subject treated. For instance, if there are 1,000 articles on a particular topic that reflect varying and opposing points of view, the investigator may select 10 or 20 of them that seem to represent the major viewpoints and conflicts opinions and/or findings. Of course, when a dissertation or thesis is involved, the expectation may be that the researcher reviews a much larger portion of literature in the final research report.

The question of how many articles should be included in a research proposal is difficult to answer in quantitative terms. If the research topic is relatively new, it is likely that little or no information exists in the available literature that bears directly on the subject. The researcher may be forced to cite available literature that is only remotely connected to the topic under investigation. For example, in the late 1950s little, if anything, was known about the impact of electronic data processing systems on school structure and administration. However, there were articles in existence that examined the impact of electronic data processing systems in petroleum refineries and airlines reservations offices. If the researcher elected to study this automation form and its impact on school systems, he would include in his review of literature information only indirectly relevant to his chosen topic. Any pioneering effort (a research project delving into previously unexplored social areas) is subject to this significant limitation. On the other hand, if there is an abundance of material in a given topic area, it is up to the researcher(s) to determine how many articles will be selected for a representative review. There are no clear-cut standards to dictate how many articles should be reviewed. Again, we return to the matter of how many are considered reasonable. Reviewing too many articles may be regarded by some researchers as superfluous activity. Other researchers may consider a particular literature review to be too scanty and inadequate. When the researcher himself feels comfortable with the articles reviewed, this subjective criterion will usually suffice.

Footnoting and referencing in literature reviews in proposals and in research reports can be handled quickly and easily by following certain conventional procedures established by such professional associations as The American Psychological

Association or The American Sociological Association. Although several footnoting and referencing styles exist, some are much more simple to follow than the others. For example, "Smith (1960: pp. 223-24) indicates that..." is considerably less awkward than "James R. Smith, PROBLEMS OF THE INNER CITY, Holt, Rinehart, and Winston, Publishers, New York, N.Y. (1960, pp. 223-24) indicates that...." Another style of footnoting is "Smith (22) indicates that...." In the first instance [i.e., Smith (1960: pp. 223-24)] a list of references consulted is provided following the proposal. The entire reference to Smith's work is included there. The second instance [i.e., Smith (22)] is indicative of a referencing system that numbers authors alphabetically.

The literature review should have an effective summary, highlighting the important findings that bear directly upon the problem to be studied. This helps the reader to understand the relationships between the various articles presented. Of course, it is assumed that the researcher has presented the articles reviewed in a coherent fashion and has woven them together meaningfully in the main presentation. A summary following their presentation will be of great value to the reader as well as the researcher.

In the quest for scientific objectivity the researcher should make every effort to present articles (particularly in controversial areas of inquiry) that represent a balanced position. Discussing articles favorable to one point of view while ignoring those favoring an opposing point of view reflects researcher bias. This practice should be avoided because it is misleading and contrary to the canons of science.

Theoretical Structure and/or Conceptual Scheme

In a sense this section of the research proposal is the heart of it. This is where the researcher formulates and develops an explanation for the relationships between the variables he is investigating. How does it come to be so that variables X and Y are associated with one another? Not only are the variables

X and Y defined here, but their logical connection is delineated. Included here are the assumptions, propositions, and definitions the researcher uses to develop the explanatory framework upon which the entire research project rests. Subsequent research will either support or fail to support the existing theoretical framework presented here.

Hypotheses

Hypotheses are logically deduced from the theoretical framework above. Within the context of the research proposal, hypotheses may be viewed as specific statements of theory in testable form. There is no limit to the number of hypotheses that can be derived from the theoretical scheme and subjected to empirical test. However, it should be noted that usually the number of hypotheses (as well as their nature) coincides closely with the objectives of the project stated earlier. In other words, by subjecting the various hypotheses to empirical test, some or all of the objectives of the research project are achieved partially or fully.

Methodology

The methodology section makes explicit the study design and constitutes the "how to do it" phase. This section includes:

1. The population to be studied;
2. The type of sampling plan to be followed;
3. The size of sample to be drawn;
4. The type of instrumentation (i.e., questionnaire, interviews, participant observation, analysis of secondary sources such as statistical records, letters, autobiographies, and so on);
5. The statistics to be used (if any) (e.g., gamma, lambda, chi square, Pearson r, and the like); and
6. The type of tabular presentation (e.g., graphs, tables, charts, figures, and so on).

The methodology section is the blueprint for researcher activity and specified how the investigator intends to test the hypotheses, study the people, or describe social settings. The researcher is at liberty to choose from among a variety of data collection techniques and study designs as well as alternative approaches to the problem. Because so many options are available to the investigator in order to study the same problem, this fact has led some persons to label social research as an "art" as opposed to a body of strategies that have specific and limited applications.

Statement of Theoretical and Substantive Implications

Although some researchers seldom give thought to the relevance of their research activity theoretically and substantively, others feel more comfortable investigating topics where several *raisons d'etre* exist. If someone were to ask us the question, "So what?" at the end of our research project, what kinds of answers could we provide to demonstrate the relevance and significance of the investigation? Although there are many researchers who pursue knowledge for the sake of knowledge and give little attention to the meaningfulness of their research activity, there are others who sense an obligation to themselves and to others to defend studies they have undertaken.

Research can be assessed from several dimensions. Some people react favorably to social research if they can see immediate and direct benefits such as reducing crime, divorce rates, and psychological stress associated with urban renewal programs. Can the research help people to overcome some of their social problems? Can the results of research be of value in the solution of ecological crises? A different kind of assessment is made of social research in terms of a time dimension. Will the results of my research today be applicable 20 or even 50 years from now even though no practical value of it is apparent presently? The work of Sigmund Freud is a case in point. In his day people were quick to discard his notions of the significance of dreams, to label the id, ego, superego and libido as nonsensical. Present-day psychologists and psychiatrists (and even some sociologists) find the work of Freud not only fascinating but insightful for assisting people with various sorts of mental problems.

Research can also be assessed in terms of its theoretical value. Does this research contribute to (support or help to substantiate) existing theories of social behavior? Or does the research refute existing theoretical orientations? Couched in the context of a relation to existing social theories, research in given areas can prove to have profound significance for the nature and growth of the academic discipline.

However, it must be acknowledged that some people prefer to study a topic simply for the pleasure and interest of understanding it more fully. They are unconcerned about the opinions of others relating to the theoretical and/or practical (substantive) significance of what they do. There must be tolerance and room for all positions taken and motives reflected in the process of social inquiry.

The Pilot Study

Although it is not essential for researchers to conduct preliminary investigations of more extensive projects, it seems well worth the time and effort in many instances to conduct what is known as a *pilot study.* Pilot studies are usually considered to be trial investigations of specific research problems that will be treated more intensively at a later date. Just as various products are tested on small consumer audiences prior to large-scale manufacture, distribution, and marketing, many projected social research plans are subjected to preliminary scrutiny on a small scale. For example, if it is the intention of an investigator to study a random sample of lawyers throughout the United States, he may wish to test his data collection methods (e.g., questionnaires, interviews, and so on) on some of his lawyer friends. Or, if he is affiliated with a university or college, he may obtain the cooperation of school officials to utilize classes of prelaw students to criticize what he intends to do at a later date on a larger scale.

Prior to a study of banking personnel, Champion and Dager (1967) administered questionnaires to employees of a neighboring bank of the one designated as the final research target. Through reactions of bank personnel to the wording of questions, questionnaire length, the relevance or meaningfulness of certain items, and other things, the data collection instruments were improved and modified substantially, and the administration and completion of the research in the actual research bank setting later was quite successful. The success of the study was undoubtedly enhanced by the pilot or preliminary investigation that helped to reveal unclear questions, awkward phrasings, and ways of approaching bank personnel most strategically.

Research projects involving the expenditure of hundreds of thousands of dollars (such as those supported by the Ford Foundation, the Department of Health, Education, and Welfare, and the National Institutes for Mental Health) cannot afford to be administered without sound planning preceding them. For instance, if the U.S. Department of Defense proposed to study factors that would influence National Guardsmen to reenlist once their military obligations were technically fulfilled, one or two National Guard units might be selected for a preliminary investigation prior to implementing a study involving hundreds of units and a substantial outlay of research funds. If the results or findings from the smaller National Guard aggregate appeared to be promising, then a better decision could be made to conduct a similar study on a larger proportion of guardsmen throughout the country.

If researchers are going to use interviewers to obtain information, they will want to include the best interviewers available within their budgetary limitations. By the same token, if they plan to use questionnaires as a primary means of data collection from a designated population, it will enhance the value and meaningfulness of their study if they are able to administer measuring instruments that focus clearly on salient characteristics of the group under investigation. Obtaining the reactions of a smaller sample of people who parallel the characteristics of those to be examined more intensively and on a larger scale at a later date will help to uncover potential weaknesses and flaws in the construction and content of the measuring instruments as well as illuminating various problems of approaching the target group and studying it most effectively.

A pilot study may be simple or complex. Its degree of elaboration and sophistication rest primarily on the standards, interests, and budget of the researcher involved. For example, many graduate student projects do not allow for extensive prestudy investigations. The resources of the study and/or his department may not allow for much preliminary testing of major study plans. The student (and often the professor) finds himself in the position of seeking assistance from other students regarding pilot studies and pretests. Granted, the preliminary administration of a questionnaire to a captive audience such as a class of introductory sociology students may not be the best way to determine potential weaknesses and flaws in study designs and the adequacy of measures, particularly if the design is directed toward a physician population. How capable are students of having empathy for physician roles? How capable are they of knowing what to regard as salient material to be included and what should be classified as irrelevant, meaningless, and therefore excluded? This problem is not easily overcome even by eliciting responses from a group paralleling the final target of inquiry (i.e., physicians). The investigator must learn to expect that no matter how flawless he flawless he believes his research plans to be, there will inevitably be those elements in the target sample who will regard their participation in any social project to be a waste of time, an annoyance, and an inconvenience. They will also likely be critical of questions that were improved on in an earlier pilot investigation with a parallel audience. In the final analysis, however, some initial pretest or pilot research activity is strongly recommended, regardless of the degree of similarity or dissimilarity between the group to be studied as the real thing and the group selected for the trial run.

It should be noted that a pilot study may make or break a projected research plan of larger scope. In view of what is uncovered in a preliminary investigation, a researcher may decide that little or nothing is to be gained through the implementation of a larger study. Many studies appearing in contemporary trade journals (e.g., *American Sociological Review, American Journal of Sociology, Social Forces, Administrative Science Quarterly,* and the like) are summaries of pilot research rather than reports of more extensive inquiry. In these instances, the investigator may quietly terminate the original plan and settle for an analysis of data collected from the smaller project.

On the other hand, many pilot studies show encouraging results, and more sophisticated research plans are implemented subsequently. Of course, we must not rule out the possibility that a sponsoring agency or funding foundation may alter or even discontinue research in particular topic areas as political changes at higher administrative levels occur. In this instance, the researcher finds himself knee-deep in a proper for which funding has been eliminated or substantially curtailed. These contingencies must always be considered as factors that could seriously affect the nature, direction, and/or the continuation of social inquiry.

Some Specific Functions of Pilot Studies

Any pilot study, regardless of the type of research involved and/or the intended target population, generally fulfills one or more of the following functions:

1. **Pilot studies help to discover and ameliorate mechanical problems associated with interviews,** *questionnaires, and the*

like. If persons are to be queried by interviewers or through self-administered questionnaires, potential problems may be spotted such as unclear wording of questions, too lengthy questionnaires or interview sessions, irrelevant and/or offensive material, poorly printed questionnaires (if questionnaires are used), and omissions of topics that should have been included initially.

2. **Pilot studies assist in developing better approaches to target populations.** Researchers are usually interested in developing and maximizing rapport with respondents under any kind of data collection condition, whether it be door-to-door interviewing or anonymous mailed questionnaires. Introductory statements by interviewers or cover letters attached to questionnaires frequently have much to do with the kind of responses elicited by respondents. For example, in a pilot study of questionnaire response rate and social class, Champion and Sear (1969, p.339) found that such things as type of postage used, type of cover letter (either an altruistic appeal or an egoistic one), and socioeconomic status of target respondents significantly affected the rate of mailed questionnaire returns from 2,700 randomly selected residents of three southern cities.

3. **Pilot studies help researchers to develop meaningful methods of categorizing data to be collected.** Problems of categorizing data occur primarily when researchers ask open-end questions or use content analysis of such documents as newspapers, letters, or diaries. In a particular election year, for example, a researcher might wish to examine the differential amounts of newspaper space devoted to covering opposing political candidates. He will have to resolve problems as to whether or not the coverage of each candidate is favorable, neutral, or unfavorable. He will also have to determine other categories by which the material extracted from the newspapers can be classified.

Equally difficult problems are encountered by researchers

as they attempt to decipher lengthy replies from respondents to open-end questions (i.e., questions that request the respondent to elaborate on his attitudes and opinions on certain issues or toward specific people). A preliminary study may sensitize the investigator to recurrent attitudinal expressions that will enable him to categorize more easily at a later date.

4. **One of the most important functions of pilot studies is to help the researcher to determine whether or not a more substantial investigation of the same phenomenon is warranted.** It may be that a projected study contains provisions for selecting a sample of inmates from a nearby penitentiary. A preliminary investigation may reveal that permission to study these inmates will not be granted. Or, if such permission is granted, subsequent refusals on the part of inmates to participate in the researcher's study will tend to discourage further investigations, at least in that particular setting.

Pilot studies can provide the researcher with important clues to the potential significance of his ideas for explaining particular social problems. If a pilot study is relatively unproductive and fails to support the investigator's explanatory framework or theory, the larger study may be scrapped. Many universities offer their professors limited funds for mini-studies. If an application for a mini-grant is approved by the appropriate university officiating body, the professor has an opportunity to explore some of his ideas on a small scale. Mini-grants may range from $100 to $5,000 or more, but they are usually fairly small. If the professor obtains positive or favorable results from his preliminary investigations supported by the mini-grant, he is in a more strategic position for applying for more substantial grants ($75,000 to $500,000) from federal or private funding agencies or foundations.

Summary

The purpose of this chapter has been to acquaint the student of social research with some of the preliminary problems associated with formulating social scientific investigations. Accordingly, research designs were defined and their objectives outlined. Specific research designs such as surveys and case studies were treated briefly with examples illustrating their respective applications in social research. In addition, several designs incorporating controls (i.e., experimental designs) were discussed, and some of their respective advantages and disadvantages were presented.

Finally, a general format for a research proposal was presented as a prerequisite to general social research projects. The pilot study was included as a a preliminary step in the preparation for more extensive and elaborate research work.

The problems of hypothesis testing, measurement of social and/or psychological variables, and some of the strategies for determining the validity and reliability of social measuring instruments. Each of these topics constitutes an integral part of the research process and must be considered as an important link in social investigation chains.

REVIEW QUESTIONS

1. Differentiate between exploratory and descriptive research designs. What are some major advantages and disadvantages of each. Identify three hypothetical (or real) instances from your own experience where these study designs would be appropriate.
2. What are some important functions associated with a research proposal? Can a researcher be too detailed in the construction and elaboration of a research proposal? Discuss why or why not.
3. People are often divided concerning whether to use case study designs or survey designs in their research activity. What to you see as contrasting advantages (and disadvantages) of each relative to the other? Discuss these briefly.
4. Define and discuss three types of experimental designs. In each case, cite their respective weakness and strengths with respect to hypothesis tests.
5. What is an experimental research design? Is it necessarily

better than exploratory and descriptive research designs in the investigation of social problems? Why or why not? Discuss.

6. What are some important objectives of pilot studies? Should they always be conducted prior to the implementation of a major research project? Why or why not? What are some potential results of conducting pilot studies?
7. What is the "classical experimental design?" What kinds of modifications have been made in relation to it which increase the flexibility of the researcher as he seeks associations between variables?

REFERENCES

Argyris, Chris. "Some Problems in Conceptualizing Organizational Climate: A Case Study of a Bank," *Administrative Science Quarterly*, 2 1958: 501-520.

Backstrom, Charles H., and Gerald D. Hursh. *Survey Research*. Evanston, Ill: Northwestern University Press, 1963.

Champion, Dean J., and Edward Z. Dager. "Some Impacts of Office Automation upon Status, Role Change, and Depersonalization," Sociological Quarterly, 8 1967: 71-84.

Chinoy, Ely. Automobile Workers and the American Dream. Garden City, N.Y.: Doubleday, 1955.

Clausen, Aage R. "Response Validity in Surveys," *Public Opinion Quarterly*, 32 1969: 588-606.

Davis, Fred. "The Cabdriver and His Fare: Facets of a Fleeting Relationship," *American Journal of Sociology*, 65 1959: 158-165.

Dean, John P., and William Foote Whyte. "How do you Know if the Informant is Telling the Truth?," *Human Organization*, 17, 1958: 34-38.

Goode, William J., and Paul K. Hatt. *Methods in Social Research*. New York: McGraw-Hill, 1952.

Hagedorn, Robert, and Sanford Labovitz. *Introduction to Social Research*. New York: McGraw-Hill, 1971.

Hyman, Herbert. *Survey Design and Analysis*. Glencoe, Ill.: The Free Press, 1955.

Kirk, Roger E. Experimental Design: *Procedures for the Behavioral Sciences*. Belmont Calif.: Brooks/Cole Publishing Co., 1968.

Selltiz, Clarie, Marie Jahoda, Morton Deutsch, and Stuart W. Cook. *Research Methods in Social Relations*. New York: Holt, 1959.

Sewell, William H., and Vimal P. Shah. "Social Class, Parental Encouragement, and Educational Aspirations," American Journal of Sociology, 73 1968: 559-572.

White, Lynn C. "Maternal Employment and Anxiety Over Mother Roles," *L.S.U. Journal of Sociology*, 2 1972: 61-81.

Whyte, William Foote. *Human Relations in the Restaurant Industry.* New York: McGraw-Hill, 1948.

CHAPTER 5

Sample Design

Tactful sample design only leads to fruitful completion of research. Research needs sufficient and accurate data. In order to procure these data a researcher conducts investigation into a given universe. Statistical data can be collected either by census enquiry or by sample enquiry. In a census enquiry all the units of a universe are studied whereas in a sample enquiry only selected number of units are observed and conclusions are drawn about the universe from their study. Many difficulties are faced in a census enquiry, particularly when the field of enquiry is large. A sample enquiry is mere adaptable than a census enquiry, because in it a small number of trained investigators can collect the whole data whereas in a census inquiry a large number of investigators may have to be appointed. It is difficult to give a proper training to a large number of investigators and as such data collected by them not always be very dependable. Besides this a sample enquiry needs comparatively less time and money.

Sample surveys are also advocated for the reason that census inquiries are in many cases either impossible or unnecessary. Thus to find out the production of wheat in India, census enquiry is more or less impossible. Besides, the census enquiry involves a great deal of time, money and energy. A proper procedure is adopted for evaluating sample plan in order to select representative units so that the influence of change and probability can be estimated. The selected respondents constitute a sample and the selection process is called 'sampling technique' or 'sampling design.'

Objectives of Sampling

The following are the major aims of sampling—

1. The prime object of sampling is to get the desired information about the universe with a prescribed reliability at the minimum cost or with the maximum reliability at a given cost.
2. The data collected should be precise and reliable which can be attained through the sampling technique.
3. The aim of sampling studies is to obtain the best possible values of the parameters. The aim is best achieved if the sample studies are made in such a way that they disclose a mathematical relationship between the values of the distribution.

Sampling Design Steps

A researcher must pay attention the following points while selecting or developing a sample design :—

1. Universe Type

The first step in developing any sample design is to clearly define the objects of the sampling known as the universe to be studied. Broadly speaking the universes can be of two types : finite and infinite. By finite universe means such populations which contain a definite number of units. Thus the number of students in the Indian universities is a finite universe. Similarly the population of the Indian universities is a finite universe.

Contrary to it an infinite universe is one in which the number of units is infinite. The length of leaves of a tree, height distribution of the Indian population or the production of rice in India would give us infinite universes.

Universes are also classified as hypothetical and existent. Hypothetical universe is one which does not consist of concrete objects.

2. Source List

Also called as 'sampling frame' from which sample is to be drawn, it contains the names of all items of a universe especially in case of a finite universe only. In case of non-availability of such source list, the researcher has to prepare it. This list should be *comprehensive, reliable, correct and appropriate.* It is extremely essential for the source list that it should represent the universe as a whole.

3. Sampling Unit

Sampling unit may be of various types. For example it may be a geographical one such as state, district, village, etc., or a construction unit such as house, flat, etc. or it may be a social unit such as family, club, school etc. The Researcher has to take the decision regarding the units that he has to select for his research study.

4. Parameters of Interest

In developing a sample design, one must consider the question of the specific population parameters which are of interest. Parameters indicate various statistical measures like mean, standard deviation, correlation etc. in the universe. There may also be important sub-groups in the population about whom estimates are made.

5. Size of Sample

The selection of the size of a sample poses a problem before a researcher. The size of sample should neither be excessively large nor too small. The size should be optimum; such size of sample should meet the requirements of efficiency, representativeness, flexibility and reliability. The precision of sample and acceptable confidence level for the estimate are things to be taken while selecting the size of sample. The larger the size of population usually the bigger sample is needed. The Parameter of the research study must be kept in view, while deciding the size of the sample.

6. Organisation of Data

The data collection, classification, editing, tabulation and studying the material are involved in the organisation of data.

7. Budgetary Provision

Cost considerations from practical point of view have an important impact upon the size of sample and its type. This may also affect to such an extent that it may even lead to the use of a non-probability sample.

8. Sampling Precedure

The last step is that the researcher should decide the type of sample he is going to select. In other words, he should decide the technique to be used in selecting the items for the sample. There is a large number of sampling designs out of which the researcher has to select for his research study. Keeping in view the cost, time and energy he should also see that the error is minimised in the sample design.

Salient Features of a Good Sample Design

The following are the salient features of a good sample design—

1. It should be free from random sampling error.
2. Sample design must be a truly representative sample.
3. It should be free from error due to bias.
4. Sample design must be viable in the context of funds available for the research study.
5. It should not suffer from incomplete coverage of units.
6. As far as possible, independent units are included in the sample.
7. Sample study can be applied in general for which such a sampling design is to be selected.

Sample Designs: Types

There are different types of sample designs based on two factors viz. the representation basis and the element selection methods. On the basis of representation, the sample may be either probability sampling or non-probability sampling. Probability sampling is based on the principle of random selection whereas non-probability sampling is 'non-random sampling.' The concept of probability is very much useful in selecting a sample from the population and helps to know the choice of degree of likeness between the sample and the population. In other words, it helps to know the probability of the sample being taken from a given universe. For example, what is the probability of selecting a sample of ten persons from the universe of persons consisting of earning members. The frequency of different income classes viz. upto Rs. 5000 and above Rs. 5000 and alike is to be examined and put them for selection by random method. Then pick up ten cards with the number of persons of the universe written by lottery method in case of non-probability or deliberate sampling or judgement representing most effectively. In this method some criterion of selection is first laid down and items are selected in accordance with it.

The following are the methods of probability sampling:

1. Simple Random Sampling.
2. Cluster Sampling.
3. Stratified Random Sampling.

Similarly Non-probability sampling of the following methods :—

1. Systematic Sampling
2. Incidental or Accidental Sampling
3. Judgement Sampling
4. Quota Sampling

5. Purposive Sampling
6. Self-selected Sampling.
7. Convenience or Chunk Sampling

1. Simple Random Sampling

A simple procedure of drawing a sample from a given universe, in this sampling each unit has an equal chance of being selected. It is also called an equal probability sampling. The process of selection is a random one but in practice we note that random sample usually is a representative sample and gives reasonably accurate data. Random sampling ensures the Law of Statistical Regularity which state that if on an average the sample chosen is a random one, the sample will have the same composition and characteristics as the universe.

Random sampling is considered as the best technique of selecting a representative sample on account of this characteristics. The salient features of simple random sampling are—

(i) This sampling technique gives each element in the population an equal probability of getting into the sample and all choice are independent of one another.

(ii) It gives each possible sample combination an equal probability of being chosen.

In simple random sampling the population units are denoted as p^1, ^{2}, p^3, p^4.......pN and sample units as s^1, s^2........sn. Where N and n denote the size of population and sample respectively. A random sample of say six units may be x^4, x^{20}, x^{5}, x^{20}, x^{25} and x^{30} or any such sample. It is obvious that $s^1=x^4$ $s^2=x^{20}$, $s^3=x^{5}$, $s^4=x^{20}$ and $s^5=x^{25}$ and $s^6=x^{30}$. The probability of selection of each unit is 1/N at the first draw 1/N-1 at the second draw, 1/N-2 at the third draw and so on.

The simple random sampling is conducted in two different ways namely simple random sampling without replacement and simple random sampling with replacement. In the former case repetitions are not possible while in the latter are.

Simple random sampling requires only a minimum knowledge of the universe in advance, it is free of error in classification but the selection of sample does not become representative. The technique is not applicable when the units are heterogeneous in nature.

2. *Cluster Sampling*

This method refers to selection of clusters or group instead of individuals units. It is adopted when the total area of interest happens to be a big one. A sample can be taken by dividing the area into a number of smaller non-everlapping areas and with the help of random technique the unit from each area are selected representing these areas or clusters. It consists of two stages : firstly, cluster elements are so formed as to include in a single cluster and secondly, a given number of clusters are shown randomly to form the sample. Clusters may or may not be equal in size of the cluster, the greater will be the precision of estimate for a given size of the sample. For instance, there are 20,000 households in a city and it is needed to select a sample of 350 households. The universe of the city is divided into wards and ensures the location of each household in these wards. If 400 such households have been identified and the average number of households in each ward is 50 (20,000/400), then select 10 wards from among 400 identified wards to constitute a sample of 350 households. The primary sampling unit remains a household.

Because of much easier and less expensive in selecting the units from the cluster or area the cluster sampling is economical. It consists of the units of both random and stratified sampling. It is less precise than random sampling.

3. *Stratified Random Sampling*

Sometimes a mixture of the two methods may give the

best possible results. The selection of sample under this technique requires prior knowledge of the universe. The universe may be divided into strata and then from each stratum some units may be selected by random sampling. The stratified random sampling consists of the following steps—

(i) The universe is stratified according to the chosen control factors.

(ii) A separate random sample is drawn from all the units of each stratum.

(iii) Mean is computed separately for each sample and is appropriately weighted to estimate universe parameter.

(iv) Variance is calculated for each sample separately in order to estimate population variance.

Thus, this sampling method means a number of random samples, one from each stratum of the universe. Instead, it is a composite of several random samples. Suppose, the universe is divided into four groups and their respective sizes being ten percent of the universe and a sample of 100 is drawn, the proportion of sample may be obtained as under:

Stratum	*Population*	*Percentage of sample*	*Sample*
First	100	10	10
Second	200	10	20
Third	300	10	30
Fourth	400	10	40

In disproportionate stratified random sampling an equal number of units is taken from each stratum regardless of the stratum represented in the universe. Thus, in the above example an equal number of units, i.e. 25 from each stratum may be drawn.

Under stratified sampling no unit/group remains unrepresented. A few units would serve the purpose in case of a perfectly homogenous stratum.

When the sizes of different strata are unequal attainment of correct population becomes difficult and improper stratification may lead to bias in the sample.

Systematic Sampling

Systematic sampling is one in which every Nth item (example every 10th item) is selected in a list representing the universe. The number of 'N' is called sampling interval. The first unit is selected at random and the remaining units are selected automatically in a predetermined manner. For example, we take a systematic sample of five households from a block of 100 households on random. First the number of households are listed out and then the 100 are divided into five. It means every 20th house holds would be selected. First household is selected from the number one to twenty. Suppose the number fifth is selected. Then of selection of every fifteenth household beginning with fifth household comes to 5, 25, 45, 65, 85 to complete the sample. This type of sampling is also known as sampling by regular intervals or sampling by fixed intervals.

Quota Sampling

Under this type of sampling technique the interviewer is instructed to collect information from an assigned number of quota of individuals in each of the several groups. The group may be specified on basis of some characteristics such as sex, age, income or others. This sampling design is very much popular in market surveys and public opinion polls. It is cheaper than random sampling. However, it lacks representativeness as the interviewer may select people according to his own convenience.

Incidental Sampling

In case of an incidental sampling, researcher picks up the cases that fall to hand continuing the process till the size of the sampling. For instance, the researcher takes 100 persons he meets on any one of the path of a street who are ready to be interviewed. For example, a sales officer of Bombay

Dyeing wants to get some generalisation about the articles of the company. He may select some people for interview conveniently available from different walks of life viz. teachers, workers, wholesalers, retailers etc. This sampling may also be called 'accidental sampling.'

Judgement Sampling

In order to have good judgement on the basis of sampling the judgement sampling is taken by an investigator with an appropriate strategy. For example, if a sample of 10 students is to be selected from a class of 100 for analysis the smoking habits of students, the investigator would select ten students who in his opinion represent the class.

Purposive Sampling

Under this sampling technique the items of the sample are selected in accordance with some purposive principle. Here the probability of the inclusion of some units of the universe in the sample is very high, while the probability of the inclusion of other very low. In this method some criterion of selection is first laid down and items are selected in accordance with it.

Convenience Sampling

When convenient population is selected for sampling design, it is called convenience sampling. In other words, under this sampling technique any part of population is selected by the researcher either by probability or by judgement or by convenience. For example, a sample obtained from automobile registrations, telephone directories etc, is convenience sample and not a random sample. It is also called 'chunk' sampling.

Self-Selected Sampling

Under this sampling technique, sample is not selected by the researcher but the member of the universe or population offer themselves for selection. For example, an enquiry has to be made about the people's opinion about Vimal Cloths; to this effect an advertisement is made in the daily newspaper asking the people to volunteer themselves to participate in the study. The people who are interested they come forward on their own to act as subjects of the study.

Sequential Sampling

It is somewhat complex sample design. The ultimate size of the sampling under this technique is not predetermined. It is determined according to mathematical decision rules on the basis of the information yielded with the progress of survey. It is used in case of statistical quality control. Lots are either accepted or rejected. When a particular lot is to be accepted or rejected on the basis of a single sample, it is called a single sampling. When the acceptance or rejection of a lot is based on two samples, it is called double sampling and when the lot of articles is accepted or rejected on the basis of more than two samples, the sampling is known as multiple sampling. Thus under this sampling design one can go on taking samples one after another as long as one desires to do so.

Conclusion

We have discussed various sample designs, we can say that normally a researcher should resort to simple random sampling because under it bias is generally eliminated and the sampling error can be estimated. But in case of small universe and its intensive study, purposive sampling is considered more appropriate. In real life there are instances when the simple random design is not used and other type of sample design is selected for solving the research problem. Hence while selecting any sample design the purpose, reliability, accuracy etc. alongwith the costs (time, money and energy) should be taken into account by the researcher.

CHAPTER 6

Research Tools

Many devices can be applied for collecting data. The instruments employed for collecting data are known as tools. The selection of suitable instruments or tools is of vital importance for carrying out successful research.

The major tools research in education can be classified broadly into the four categories viz. Inquiry forms; observation; sociometry; and psychological tests.

1. Inquiry Forms
   - (a) Questionnaire
   - (b) Schedule
   - (c) Check-List
   - (d) Rating Scale
   - (e) Score Card
   - (f) Opinionnaire or Attitude Scale
2. Observation
3. Sociometry
4. Psychological Tests
   - (a) Achievement Test
   - (b) Aptitude Test
   - (c) Intelligence Test
   - (d) Interest Inventory
   - (e) Personality Measures.

1. Inquiry Forms

Inquiry forms are a class of data-gathering devices which make use of properly prepared proforma or forms for inquiry into and securing information about certain phenomena under study. Admist many such inquiry forms, perhaps the most used and the most abused is the 'Questionnaire'.

QUESTIONNAIRE

Goode and Hatt (1952) state "In general the word questionnaire' refers to a device for securing answers to questions by using a form which the respondent fills in himself."

It is aprt to quote Barr, Davis and Johnson (1953) who define questionnaire as "a systematic compilation of questions that are submitted to a sample of population from which information is desired."

A questionnaire is used when factual information is required. An opinionnaire or attitude scale is used when opinions rather than facts are desired. It is an important instrument in normative survey research to gather information from widely scattered sources. It is the most flexible of tools in collecting both quantitative and qualitative information. A properly constructed and administered questionnaire may serve as a most appropriate and useful data gathering device.

Questionnaires administered personally to groups of individuals have a number of advantages.

1. The person administering the instrument has an opportunity to establish direct rapport, explain the purpose of the study and explain the meaning of items that may sometimes be not clear.
2. The availability of a number of respondents in one place makes possible an economy of time and expenses and provides a high proportion of useful responses for research.

The persons from distant places and who cannot be personally contacted mailed questionnaire may be useful. The mailed questionnaire is one of the most used and probably most criticised data-gathering device. It has been referred to as the lazy person's way of gaining information, although the careful preparation of a good questionnaire takes a great deal of time, hard work and ingenuity.

Most often questionnaires sent out by the fresh researchers suffer from certain errors with the result that the reaction to questionnaires is often unfavourable and response is slow, scanty and frequently disappointing, providing a very flimsy basis for generalisation.

A questionnaire may have the following common errors:

(i) Questionnaires are very often too lengthy.

(ii) The form is poorly drafted and organised.

(iii) The items are vaguely worded or improperly arranged; and

(iv) The subject is of trivial importance

Forms of Questionnaire

Mainly the questionnaires can be of the following types:

(i) *Structured vs. Non-structured Questionnaire*: The structured contains definite, concrete and directed questions, whereas non-structured may of partially completed questions or statements. A non-structured questionnaire is often used as the interview guide, which is non-directive. The interviewer possesses only a blueprint of the enquiries and he is largely free to arrange the form or statements of the questions. But in a structured questionnaire the statements, the items and their seriation etc. are prefixed and they are used in the same manner.

(ii) *Fact and Opinion Questionnaires* : Questionnaire of fact require certain information of facts from the respondent without any reference to his opinion or attitude about them whereas in the questionnaire of opinion and attitude informant's opinion, attitude or preference regarding some phenomena is sought.

(iii) *Closed vs. Open Questionnaire* : Sometimes referred

to as the "restricted" or "structured" type, the closed from questionnaire consists of a question or statement to which a person responds by selecting one or more choices already given, such as "yes" or "no" or alternative responses. Here the candidate marks a `yes' or `no,' write a short response, or check an item from a list of responses suggested.

Generally satisfactory, the closed form questionnaire is easy to fill out, takes little time, keeps the respondent on the subject, is relatively objective, and is fairly easy to analyse and tabulate.

The open form, "open end" or "unrestricted" or "free response" (as this is known) type questionnaire calls for a free response in the respondents's own words. The respondent frames and supplies his own response. No clues are provided. It probably provides for greater depth of response. The type of item is sometimes difficult to interpret, tabulate and summarise in the research report. The responses may be too brief also, or the respondent may have ignored important information on the theme.

Most questionnaires include both open and closed type items. Each type of these items has merits and limitations and the questionnaire framer must decide which type is more likely to elicit the information required. The appropriateness of the recall and recognition items for eliciting different kinds of information should be determined.

Salient Features of Good Questionnaire

1. It is reasonably short, though comprehensive enough to secure all relevant information.
2. The covering letter is written in a friendly tone and it indicates its importance.
3. It has straightforward, clear and complete directions.
4. Each item (question) deals with single idea in simple terms.

5. It does not seek information which may be obtainable from other sources.
6. It is attractive in appearance, neatly arranged, clearly duplicated and free from typographical errors.
7. The offending, annoying or embarrassing questions have to be avoided as far as possible.
8. Allow code numbers for all possible responses to permit easy transference to machine tabulation card.
9. Questions do not contain leading suggestions for the respondents and are objective in nature.
10. Putting two questions in one question are also avoided.
11. They are so worded, that it is easy to tabulate and interpret the responses.
12. Descriptive adjectives, and adverbs that have no agreed upon meanings are avoided, e.g. words like frequently, occasionally, rarely etc.
13. Questions are presented in good psychological order proceeding from general to more specific responses.
14. Double negatives are also avoided, e.g. Don't you disapprove of forced discipline?

Guidelines for Construction of a Questionnaire

1. Get all the help you can and make all preparation for planning and constructing your questionnaire.
2. Submit your questionnaire items for criticism to your friends and colleagues.
3. Follow the following principles:
   (a) Be careful of inadequate alternatives.
   (b) Underline a word if you wish to indicate special emphasis.
   (c) For ratings and comparisons a point of reference is necessary.
   (d) Define or qualify terms that could easily be misinterpreted.

(e) Phrase questions so that they suit all respondents.
(f) Minimise the effect of certain conditions which impair reliability and validity.
(g) Avoid unwarranted assumptions.
(h) Design the items with a view to quantify the result.
(i) Design questions that will give a complete response.

4. Take into consideration the situation in which the average respondent works.
5. Avoid overlapping of items in different sections.
6. Try the questionnaire on a few representatives of the population. Improve the items.
7. Study other questionnaires, and keep in mind the characteristics of a good questionnaire.
8. On the whole, the questionnaire as a research tool should be brief, sharply focussed on its specific purpose, and explanatory of what, why, who, for whom and how.
9. Consider the psychology of the respondents to see how their attention, sympathy and cooperation can be secured.
10. Eliminate irrelevant items and make the questionnaire as brief as possible.
11. The problem under investigation, and the topic of the questionnaire, must be of sufficient significance to motivate subjects to respond.
12. The problem must be defined in terms of specific objectives concerning the kind of information needed; specific hypotheses or questions must be formulated and every items on the questionnaire should directly relate to them.
13. Subjects should be selected using an appropriate

sampling technique (or an entire population may be used), and identified subjects must be persons who (a) have the desired information and (b) are likely to be willing to give it.

14. If the response rate is below 70% better use interview or observation technique.

Advantages

1. As an instrument of science, the questionnaire has great potentialities when it is properly used.
2. It is an economical way of information accumulation of significance to educators in terms of time, effort and cost.
3. In comparison to use of an interview procedure, a questionnaire is much more efficient and permits collection of data from a much larger sample. It permits a nationwide or even international coverage.
4. It permits group administration.
5. It is easy to plan, construct and administer.
6. It is dependable to obtain statements of facts.
7. Personal information may be obtained more readily by means of questionnaire.
8. It places less pressure on the subject for immediate response.
9. It helps in focussing the respondent's attention on all the significant items. In a written form its standardised instructions for recording responses ensure some uniformity.
10. It may be used as a preliminary tool for conducting a depth study later on by any other method.

Limitations

1. It gives a prejudiced sample. The matter of non-response is always a big question mark.

2. It is impossible to put down certain delicate and confidential issues in writing.
3. Frequently questionnaire research is compilation of the opinions of many persons who do not know the answer.
4. The questionnaire cannot be used with illiterate subjects and young children.
5. The respondents may not constitute a representative sample of the entire group.
6. Some times the responses are not true, factual and honest and original.
7. If the subject misinterprets a question or gives an incomplete or indefinite response, nothing can be done whereas in an interview questions can be rephrased and clarified.
8. It is not very helpful in delicate and controversial issues and in penetrating the subject's feelings and sentiments.
9. The questionnaire does not provide any opportunity to the investigator to establish rapport with the subject.

Depite above limitations, still the use of questionnaire is much favoured and popular. It serves a very useful and definite purpose in research. There is need for the improvement of its quality and its judicious use.

SCHEDULE

Goode and Hatt (1952) are of the opinion that, "Schedule is the name usually applied to a set of questions which are asked and filled in by an interviewer in a face to face situation with an other person." A schedule is different from a questionnaire in that the former is administered personally to a respondent or a group of respondents while the latter is usually mailed. The schedule provides opportunity to establish rapport, to explain the purpose and to make the meaning to items clear. It also economises time and expense and provides complete information and usually returned.

A schedule differs from an interview because it is only a part of the interview and not the whole of it. The pre-planned questions to be asked by the interviewer is only one part of the total process of interview.

A schedule suffers from some lacunae too. It may not be possible to contact all the respondents personally. Or the personal contact may prove to be too expensive or time consuming. The substitutes that can safely be used in place of the schedule are the mailed questionnaire or check list.

The characteristics of a good schedule, the ways of constructing, the analysis, the interpretation of data gathered through a schedule are not very different from those of a questionnaire.

However, its administration in a face to face situation is different from the administration of questionnaire, which is to be done by the investigator as he would ask his questions in an interview.

CHECK-LIST

The check-list is a simple laundry-list of device, consisting of a prepared list of items. It is a type of questionnaire in the form of a set of categories for the respondent to check. It is used to record the presence or absence of the phenomenon under study. Responses are the facts and not the judgement. The tool was the advantage of systematising and facilitating the recording of observations and of helping to assure the consideration of all important aspects of the object or act observed.

The check list is an important tool in gathering facts for educational surveys. It may also be used as a form of recording in observational studies of behaviour. When used as a sort of scale to yield a score, it is an instrument often used in educational appraisal studies of school building property, plan, text-books, instructional procedures and results etc.

Guidelines for Constructing a Check-List

1. Closely examine closely some good check-lists prepared by successful researchers.
2. Read many descriptions on the construction and use of check-lists in educational research.
3. Determine the items on which you require information for your study and details you need.
4. Arrange the items in categories of logical and psychological orders. Related items should be grouped together.
5. Arrange the individual items in an adequate way to secure the information and details you require. Check list items can be arranged in many ways. Four common styles of arrangement as suggested by Homer and Kempfer (1960) are:

   (i) The form in which items are positive statements with checks (✓) to be marked in a column on the right.

   (iu) The form where items can best be embedded in sentences and the appropriate word is checked, underlined or encircled.

   (iii) that which asks that all items found in a situation be checked.

   (iv) The form in which questions with a 'yes/no' are asked to be encircled, underlined or checked in response to the items given.

   One may choose the style appropriate to one's subjects and queries. It may be one or more than one style.
6. Check lists must be complete and comprehensive. A pilot study and survey of previous literature is helpful in this direction.

7. To improve the validity of the check-list phrase the items in such a way that they are discriminative in quality. The definitions of the items be carefully written in.

Analysis and Interpretation of Check-List Data

The tabulation and quantification of check list data is done in very much the same way as of the questionnaire responses. Frequencies are counted, percentages and averages calculated, means, medians and coefficients of correlation computed as and when required. In long check-lists, the checks are added up. Total scores for different categories can be compared. Finally the conclusions should be drawn in most judicious way.

RATING SCALE

Definition

"Rating is a term applied to expression of opinion or judgement regarding some situation, object or character. Opinions are usually expressed on a scale of values. Rating techniques are devices by which such judgements may be quantified." (Barr and Davis, 1953).

The rating scale is a very useful device is assessing quality—especially when quality is difficult to measure objectively. For example, "How good was the performance?" is a question which can hardly be answered objectively.

"The rating scale typically directs attention to different parts or aspects of the thing to be evaluated." (Good and Scates, 1954)

"A rating scale ascertains the degree, intensity, or frequency of a variable." (Van Dalen, 1979)

"Rating is a term applied to expression of opinion or judgement regarding some situation, object or character. Opinions are usually expressed on a scale of values, rating techniques are devices by which such judgements may be quantified." (A.S. Barr 1953)

Rating scales record judgements or opinions and indicate the *degree* or *amount*. Descriptions of different degrees of quality are arranged along a line from high to low or otherwise, and this line is the scale.

How good was the performance?

1. Excellent
2. V. Good
3. Good
4. Average
5. Below
6. Poor
7. V. Poor
8 Average

Rating scales measure the nature or degree of certain aspects or characteristics of a person or phenomenon through the use of series of numbers, qualitative terms, named attributes or verbal descriptions. They can be used for :

1. Personality rating,
2. Teacher rating,
3. School appraisal.
4. Testing the validity of instruments, etc.

A rating scale is a method by which we systematise the expression of opinion concerning a trait. The ratings are done by parents, teachers, a board of interviews and judges and by self as well.

There are two characteristics of a rating scale :

(1) Description of the characteristics to be rated, and
(2) Some methods by which the quality, frequency or importance of each items to be rated may be given.

Advantages of Rating Scales

1. Helpful in writing reports to parents.
2. Helpful in finding out students' need.
3. Helpful in supplementing other sources of undertakings about the child.
4. Helpful in making recommendations to employers.
5. Helpful in their stimulating effect upon the individuals who are rated.
6. Helpful in filling out admission blanks for colleges.

Limitations of Rating Scales

1. The average or medium rating of a number of judges is superior to that of a single judge, provided there are not great differences in the capability of judges.
2. Raters having one form of contact with the individual being rated (teachers from the same school subject) tend to agree more closely than do rate with more diversified contacts.
3. People differ markedly in their ability to make ratings.
4. People differ in their reliability as subjects for ratings.
5. Immediate emotional reactions affect ratings.
6. One tends to rate one's own sex higher than the opposite sex on desirable traits.
7. Long intimate friendship bring marked decreases in the reliability of ratings. Persons tend to over-rate intimate friends on desirable traits and under-rate less desirable traits.
8. "General all round value" is frequently more reliably rated than are some of the more specific qualities involved.
9. Self-ratings tend to be too high on desirable traits and too low on undesirable traits.
10. Raters are frequently unable to justify ratings, or, are apt to give absurd rationalisations.

"The design of the rating technique must always take into account the existence of there elements :

(i) the judges who will do the rating,

(ii) the phenomena to be rated, and

(iii) the continuum along which they will be rated.

If the design does not adequately define all these three elements then only unreliable and invalid results can be expected. All three components must be very carefully selected."

Guidelines for the Construction and Use of Rating Scales

1. Choose only the most significant aspects of a thing, trait or phenomenon of the study.
2. Set up five to seven categories in such terms as:

Superior	Above Average	Average	Fair	Inferior
Excellent	Good	Average	Below Average	Poor
Always	Frequently	Occa-sionally	Rarely	Never

3. Items may be arranged in ascending or descending order from *left* to *right*. Ordinarily an odd number of steps should be used and the average or usual quality should be kept in the middle.
4. The meaning of different qualities or adjectives used in the items should be clearly different from each other, and in going 'up' the scale one should feel that the next description represents better quality than the last.
5. The directions of using the rating scales should be clear and comprehensive.
6. At least three divisions of quality must be kept. (A two division rating scale—'Yes/No,' 'Good Bad'—forms a check list.

7. The rating scale is always composed of two parts—
   (i) an instruction which names the subject and defines the continuum, and
   (ii) a scale which defines the points to be used in rating.
8. Only well-informed and experienced persons should be selected for rating where technical competence is required.
9. The trait to be rated should be readily observable.
10. Employ several judges, depending on the rating situation, to obtain desirable reliability.
11. In the rating scale card, some space may be provided for the rater to write some supplementary material.

Common Errors in Rating

1. *Generosity Error:* Raters tend to be generally generous. It has been verified that 60% to 80% of unselected group tend to receive above average ratings in all traits. The raters are inclined to be unduly generously in rating aspects which they have no opportunity to observe. Such an error is known as generosity error.
2. *Stringency Error:* It is the opposite of generosity error. Some raters have a tendency to rate all individuals low.
3 *The Logical Error:* Such an error occurs when the characteristics or the traits to be rated are misunderstood.
(4 *The Error of Central Tendency:* There is a tendency in some observers to rate all or most of the ratees near the mid-point of the scale. They would like to put most of the ratees as 'Average' etc.
5. *The Halo Error:* 'Halo' means a tendency to rate in terms of general impressions about the ratee formed on the basis of some previous performance.

Rating Scales Types

The main types of rating scales are as follows:

(1) *Descriptive Rating:* The rater puts a check (✓) in the blank before the characteristic or trait which is described in word or phrase. In this the alternative statements/ words are already given.

(2) *Numerical Scale:* Here number are assigned to each trait. If it is a seven point scale the number '7' represents the maximum amount of that trait in the individuals, 4 represents the average amount.

(3) *The Graphic Scale:* This is similar to the descriptive scale and the difference lies only in the way it is written. This is also called "Behavioural Statement Scale." These are of two types :

   (a) *Simple Scale:* In this all the points are represented in graphic manner and show the degree of points. For example: He shows responsibility for completing work.
   - Very high
   - High
   - Average
   - Low
   - Very low

   (b) *Social Attitude Scale:* It studies the social attitude of individuals. For Example—What type of attitude that student has:
   - Anti-social
   - Self centred
   - Has no positive attutide
   - Usually considerate to others
   - Strongly altruistic

(4) *Man to Man Scale:* An individual is asked to rate the ratee by comparing him to the person mentioned on

the scale and assuming the ratee his position. For example, who out of the ABCDE, is generally a persistent person?

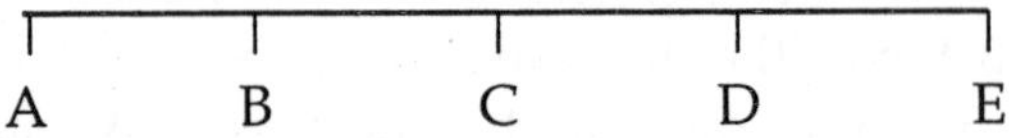

(5) *The Percentage of Group Scale:* Here the rater is asked to give the percentage of the group that possesses the trait on which the individual is rated. For example, for rating the self-confidence of an individual, the rater may check one of the following :

- Falls in the top 1%
- Falls in the top 10%, but not in the top one per cent
- Falls in the top 25%, but not in the top 10% and so on.

SCORE CARD

The score card is an elaborate form of Rating scale in which items are always evaluated, usually in numerical terms. Sometimes the two terms—score card and rating scale—are used almost interchangeably. The score card provides for the appraisal of the relatively large number of aspects. Its ratings usually yield a total weighted score and thus reach in over-all evaluation. The rater is provided with a general standard of criteria in detail and he is asked to rate only a single unit of the total situation at a time. The general practice is to employ a number of raters and their scores combined and averaged.

Score cards are frequently used in evaluating communities, building-sites, schools, text-books, socio-economic states, the worth of any educational work or institution.

Limitations of Score Cards

— Its limitations and difficulties are similar to those of rating scales.

— The difficulties of choosing, identifying and qualifying the significant aspects of the factors to be observed are real.

— The suspicion that the whole of a thing may be greater than the sum of its parts.

OPINIONNAIRE OR ATTITUDE SCALE

"An opinionnaire is defined as a special form of inquiry used by the educational researchers to collect the opinions of a sample of population on certain facts or factors the problem under investigation. These opinions on different facts of the problem under study are further quantified, analysed and interpreted."

The opinionnaire or attitude scales have been designed to measure attitudes of an individual or group of people towards issues, institutions or people (such as capital punishment, teacher training, religious education in schools, etc.).

Opinion and *Attitude* are allied but not synonymous terms. *Attitude* denotes the inner feeling or belief of a person towards a particular phenomenon. In other words how people feel, or what they believe is their attitude. But it is difficult, if not impossible, to describe and measure attitude.

Opinion is what a person says about his attitudes towards some phenomenon. It is the outward expression of an attitude held by an individual. His attitude can be inferred or estimated from his statements of opinion.

Measurement and description of opinion and attitudes is an interesting area of research where data is collected in the form of expressed opinion of individuals. To obtain the measure of the attitude or belief of an individual or a group of individuals towards some phenomenon the inquiry form called *opinionnaire* or *attitude scale* is used.

Limitations of Attitude Scale/Opinionnaire

1. They may not really known how they feel about a social issue, never having given the idea serious consideration.
2. People may conceal their attitudes and express socially acceptable opinions.
3. People may be unaware of their attitude about a situation in the abstract, until confronted with a real situation, they may be unable to predict their reaction or behaviour.
4. Observation of behaviour may not always be possible when a large sample is under study.
5. Attitudes are revealed through the behaviour of an individual. But behaviour itself is not always a true indication of attitude. Social custom or the desire for social approval makes many overt expressions of behaviour mere formalities, quite unrelated to people's inward feelings.

Characteristics of Attitude Scale/Opinionnaire

1. The opinionnaire makes use of statements or questions on different aspects of the problem on three points or five point scale, e.g.

   - Agree
   - Undecided
   - Disagree

   or

   - Strongly agree
   - Agree
   - Uncertain
   - Disagree
   - Strongly Disagree

2. It uses the favourable or unfavourable statements on different aspects of the problem in hand.
3. It may be subdivided into sections.
4. The gally poll ballots generally make use of questions instead of statements. The public opinion polls generally rely on personal contacts rather than mail ballots.

With the limitations mentioned above psychologists and sociologists have explored some methods to measure the opinion of people as closely related to their feelings or attitude. These methods are as follows:

1. Asking people directly how they feel about a subject. This technique may employ a schedule or questionnaire of the open or closed from or interview process in which the respondents express their opinion orally.
2. Asking people to check in a list the statements with which they agree.
3. Asking people to indicate their degree of agreement or disagreement with a series of statements about a controversial subject.
4. Inferring their attitudes from reactions to projectives devices, through which they may reveal attitudes unconsciously.

Indirect methods of evaluating attitudes tend, however, to be more accurate than direct methods in determining the direction and intensity of an attitude. The following procedures for eliciting opinions and attitudes have been used extensively.

1. THURSTONE TECHNIQUE OF SCALED VALUES

To measure the attitude of an individual towards a group, institution, idea or practice, a number of statements (twenty or more) expressing different points of view about the subject in question are assembled. They are than submitted to a panel of judges, each of whom arranges them in eleven groups-ranging from one extreme to another in position. Those items which bring out a marked disagreement between the judges in assigning a position are discarded. From the sorting by each judge of the items retained a composite position for each statement is calculated. The median scale value for each statement, thus calculated on the basis of the pannel judgement, falls between 1 and 11. The list of statements is than ready to be given to the subjects who are asked to check the statements with which they are in agreement. This response is quantified on the basis on the median values of the statements. This is the first method of attitude statement known as the Thurstone Technique of Scaled Values (Thurstone and Chave, 1929).

2. LIKERT METHOD

The second method—the Likert Method of Summated Ratings—can be performed without a panel of judges and has yielded scores very similar to those obtained by the Thurstone Method. The coefficient of correlation between the two scales was reported as high as +.92 in the study by Edwards and Kenney (1946). Since the Likert-type scale takes much less time to construct, it offers an interesting possibility for the student of opinion research. The Likert scale was found superior to other scales as it yielded a mean correlation coefficient of .54 with the objective indices of voting behaviour.

Likert (1932) developed this technique of scaling for helping to eliminate questionable items from the scale. The essence of the Likert technique is to increase the variation in the possible scores, by coding from "strongly agree" to "strongly disagree" instead of merely "agree" or "disagree."

A Likert Scale asks an individual to respond to a series of statements by indicating whether she or he strongly agree (SA), is undecided (U), disagree (D), or strongly disagree (SD) with each statement (Likert 1932). Each response is associated with a point value, and an individual's score is determined by summing the point values for each statement. For example, the following point values might be assigned to responses to positive statements : SA=5; A=4; U=3; D=2; SD=1. For negative statements, the point values would be reversed, that is, SA=1; A=2; and so on. An example of a positive statement might be "short people are entitled to the same job opportunities as tall people." A high point value on a positively stated item would indicate a positive attitude and a high total score on the test would be indicative of a positive attitude.

A scale score is computed for each statement. If person A makes a very high score and person B a very low score, their answers to all questions can be compared to see if there is any single question that the persons with the two very different scores answered identically. Such a question obviously does not discriminate well between discrepant scores on the concept, and so would be eliminated from the scale. For example, if person A had a score of 55 and person B a score of 3, but both had identical answers on question 7, then 7 would be dropped from the scale.

Procedure for Likert Scaling

1. Write a large number of questions thought to measure the dimensions to be scaled.
2. Select a sample of respondents representative of the population on which the scale will be used.
3. Code all responses so that a higher score on a particular item indicates a stronger agreement with the attitude being scaled (code 5 for either strong agreement with a positive statement of strong disagreement with a negative one, and code 1 for strong disagreement with a positive statement or strong agreement with a negative one); compute a scale score for each person by summing her or his scores on all questions.

4. Analyse responses and select for the scale the items most clearly differentiating between the highest and lowest scores.

The investigator can divide the respondents into quartiles and compute and median score on each item for the highest 25 per cent and the lowest 25 per cent of scale scores. If any question has the same median score for both the high and low groups it can be eliminated from the scale. Only questions that reveal widely different median scores for the highest and lowest groups will be retained. Also, each item can be correlated with the total score or with other items that discriminate well between the highest and lowest quartiles of scores. Items that do not correlate highly can be eliminated from the scale.

Limitations of Likert Scaling

1. It is somewhat inexact and fails to measure opinion with the precision one would desire.
2. There is no basis for belief that the five positions indicated on the scale are equally spaced. The interval between "strongly agree" and "agree" may not be equal to the interval between "agree" and "undecided." It is also unlikely that the statements are of equal value in "forness" or "againstness."
3. It is unlikely that the respondent can validly react to a short statement on a printed form in the absence of real-life situations.
4. It is doubtful whether equal scores obtained by several individuals indicate equal favourableness toward the given position. Actually, different combinations of positions can yield equal score values without necessarily indicating equivalent positions of attitude or opinion.
5. There is a possibility that people may answer according to what they think they should feel rather than how they do feel.

3. SEMANTIC DIFFERENTIAL METHOD

The third method of attitude assessment was developed by Osgood, Suci, and Tannenbaum (1957), known as Semantic Differential. This is similar to the Likert method in that the respondent indicates an attitude or opinion between two extreme choices. This method usually provides the individual with a seven-point scale with two adjectives at either and of the scale, such as good-bad, unhealthy-healthy, clean-dirty. The respondent is asked to rate a group, individual, or object on each of these bipolar scales.

The respondent indicates the point on the continuum between the extremes that represent her or his attitude. Based on their researches, the original developers of this approach reported that most adjective pairs represent one of three dimensions which they labelled evaluation (e.g. good-bad); potency (e.g. strong-weak), and activity (e.g. active-passive). For example, on a scale concerning attitudes towards property taxes, the following items might be included :

Necessary — Unnecessary
Fair — Unfair

In practice, however these dimensions are frequently ignored and/or replaced by other dimensions thought to be more appropriate in a particular situation.

Each position on a continuum has an associated score value, by totalling score values all items, it can be determined whether the respondent's attitude is positive or negative. Semantic differential scales usually have 5 to 7 intervals with a neutral attitude being assigned a score value of 0.

A person who checked the first interval (i.e. 3) on both of these items would be indicating a very positive attitude.

The semantic differential has limitations similar to those of the Thurstone and Likert approaches. In spite of these limitations, however, the process of opinion measurement has merit. These techniques can serve a useful purpose in social research.

4. GUTTMAN SCALING

Louis Guttman (1944) has devised a method of scaling called *scalogram analysis* that is designed to ensure that there is only one (unique) combination of responses for each different scale score. That is, while there may be ten or more different ways to make a score of 2 with Likert scaling, there is only one way to make a score of 2 on a Guttman scale. Thus a Guttman scale is more likely than a Likert scale to be unidimensional.

Guttman's scalogram analysis is cumulative in the sense that the combination of responses required to make a particular score includes the responses to all questions required to make the next lower score, plus the response to one additional question, in a stepwise fashion.

Steps

The Guttman scaling procedures beings about the same way as the summated ratings or Likert procedure:

- The researcher selects a group of items that he or she thinks should form a unidimensional scale of whatever concept he or she wishes to scale.
- In the simplest forms of scalogram analysis, only two responses are allowed for each question.
- These can be coded with any binary coding system (1 or 0; + or -; and a or b).
- These items should have face validity (they should all atleast appear to measure the concept in question).
- Have many more cases (respondents) than questions to be scaled to be make an error free scale.

A Guttman scale also asks respondent to agree or disagree with a number of statements. It, however, attempts to determine whether an attitude is unidimensional; it is unidimensional if it produces a cumulative scale. In a cumulative scale, an individual who agrees with a given statement also agrees with all related preceding statements; for example, if you agree with statement 3, you also agree with statements 2 and 1.

Advantages and Disadvantages of Guttman Scaling

— Construction of a Guttman scale is more difficult than construction of summated rating scales in the sense that former requires all items to be responded to in a certain cumulative order while the latter does not.

— It ensures that each scale score can be made in only one way, while the summated rating technique does not.

— It does not allow two different and separate combinations of responses to tie for the same rank score.

— For Guttman scaling to be proven superior to Likert scaling we must show that it is more likely to lead to unidimensionality.

Guidelines for Preparing Opinionnaire Items

1. Various individuals may be requested to express their opinions about the phenomenon orally or in writing.
2. A careful study may be made of the list of statements prepared and used for measuring attitude by the investigator in the related areas of research.
3. Statements selected should be unambiguous in their meaning through a pilot study.
4. Available literature may be surveyed thoroughly.
5. Favourable and unfavourable statements may be collected from sources.
6. Statements should be arranged in a random system irrespective of their favourable or unfavourable indications.

7. The following types of statements should be chosen: (i) Statements presenting as wide a variety of situations as possible, (ii) Statements which prevent the individual from detecting the nature of attitude which is being evaluated.
8. It is better to collect a large number of statement that are needed for the research worker for preparing an attitude scale.
9. Approximately an equal number of favourable and unfavourable statements may be selected.

CHAPTER 7
Interview Schedules

Interview schedules are the backbone of any successful research investigation. Here, we are presenting very useful information for researchers.

The schedule is the form containing some questions or blank tables which are to be filled by the workers after getting information from the informants. The schedule may thus contain two types of questions *firstly* those that are in form of direct questions and *secondly* those that are in form of a table. There are some kinds of information that can be procured only by putting a question, e.g. questions for eliciting the informants opinion, attitude, preferences or his suggestions about some matter. There are others which may better be put in form of tables. Generally most of them may be used interchangingly. Thus for knowing the nature of post held by a person, it may either be in form of a question—"what is the nature of post held by you at present", or in form of a table with heading—"Nature of post held..." Tables should be preferred to questions wherever they can conveniently be used. They are clearer to observe and easy to tabulate.

Kinds of Schedules

The schedules used in the social research may be classified into following four groups according to the use to which they are put.

1. *Relating Schedules*—They are used for sociological or psychological research vocational guidance. They are used in those cases where the attitude, or opinion is to be measured. Different ranks or scales are constructed for this purpose.

2. *Document Schedules*—These schedules are used for recording data from written documents like autobiography, case history, diary or official records mantained by the government. Such schedules are used for preparing the source list of collecting preliminary information about the universe.

3. *Interview Schedules*—Used for interview purpose, it is with these schedules that we shall be mainly concerned in this chapter. They contain standard questions that the interviewer has to ask and blank tables that he has to fill up after getting information from the respondents.

4. *Observations Schedule*—These schedules are used for observation purposes. They contain specific topics upon which the observer has to concentrate and the nature of information that he has to record. Such schedules make the observation more pointed and accurate by pointing clearly what is to be observed. How it is to be observed and how it is to be recorded. A fuller and more detailed discussion of such schedules has been given in the chapter on observation.

Purpose of Schedule

The purpose of schedule is to provide a standardised tool for observation or interview in order to attain objectivity. By schedule every informants has to reply the same questions put in the same language and the field worker has no choice to get the desired reply by putting a different question or changing the language of the same question. The order of the questions is also the same and thus the whole interview takes place under standardised conditions, and the data received is perfectly comparable. It has now been proved that responses of the people regarding the same matter differ, if the language of the question is even slightly different or even the place of question is changed. A perfectly standardised form is, therefore, needed for any objective study.

One more purpose of schedule is to act as memory tickler. In the absence of any schedule the field worker may put different number of questions to different people. He may forget to enquire about some important aspects and then he would be required to go over the whole process again to collect that missing invironment. In case of observation too, the schedule keeps his memory refreshed, and keeps him reminded of the different aspects that are to be particularly observed.

Another purpose of schedule is to facilitate the work of tabulation and analysis. When information is collected in a conversational form by means of free story method, the interview is mostly in form of a narrative, or historical account. It becomes very difficult afterwards to sort out the relevant parts and classify them into different groups for the purpose of further analysis. Moreover the classes may not be homogeneous because of the different methods of recording and different aspects observed. The schedule puts the whole thing in a structured form and tabulation and analysis become very easy. In fact the questions are formed, while keeping in mind the tabulation plan, to facilitate this work.

Salient Features Good Schedule

P.V. Young is of the opinion that, there are two essential conditions of a good schedule. (a) Accurate response; and (b) Accurate communication.

1. *Accurate response*—Accurate response is said to have been achieved when replies contain the information sought for. This information should be unbiased and true. The respondents may also co-operate in filling the schedule, by giving out correct information.

Following steps are generally taken to achieve the above two objectives:

(a) The size and physical structure of the schedule should be attractive.

(b) The questions should be clearly worded, easy to follow without any ambiguity or doubt.

(c) Right type of questions should be asked.

(d) Questions asked or information sought should be adequate and relevant to the enquiry, so that final generalisations may be based upon it.

(e) The information sought should not only be valid, it should also be capable of being tabulated and if possible being subjected to statistical analysis.

2. *Accurate Communication*—Accurate communication is achieved when respondents understand the questions in the same sense which they are expected to convey. Thus the basis of accurate communication is proper wording of questions. The questions should be so worded that they may clearly carry the desired sense without any ambiguity. Various tools for achieving accuracy of communication have been discussed in the succeeding paragraphs.

Procedure for Forming a Schedule

While devising or framing the schedule *the first question* to be asked is—"what are the different aspects of the problem." The problem under study should first of all be split up into various aspects. The determination of these aspects will depend upon clear understanding of the problem under study. Thus, for example, if the survey of the effect of employment of women upon family life is to be made the different aspects of the problem would be care of the children, household work marital relations, health, and general attitude etc. Every aspect is to be studied in complete detail.

The very next step .is to be decided "what information is necessary for a valid generalisation on each aspect." For this purpose each aspect has again to be broken up into a number of sub parts. These sub-parts should be exhaustive to give a full and complete picture of the aspect under study. To keep in view above illustration, care of the children may further be divided into care in respect of food, clothing, study, companionship, etiquettes health and habits etc. Information may be elicited about each of them.

The third step is the framing of actual questions. This part deals with the form and working of the questions. More than one questions may be asked to get complete information about the particular aspect. Care should be taken to see that the questions convey the exact sense, are easily followed by the response and they will be willing to suppy information without nay hesitation, bias or distortion of facts. When information can not be secured by direct questions, indirect questions may be resorted to. This part is the most vital part of the schedule and any error in it may invalidate the whole enquiry through biased, incorrect, incomplete or irrelevent information.

The fourth step is general layout of the schedule and arrangement of questions. When the questions have been given definite form the other problem is to arrange them in proper form. The layout or physical design of the schedule is very important. If it is well planned and attractive to look at, replies may be coming forth without hesitation. A bad, clumsy and unbalanced schedule is very difficult to fill and errors may be frequent. Various steps are taken to achieve this objective. They have been discussed in detail in the latter part of this chapter.

The last step is testing the validity of schedule. After the schedule has been prepared, it has to be tested on a sample population to find out any discrepencies left out. Whatever may be the degree of precaution taken, some slips are bound to be left out and can not be located unless the schedule has been put into operation. Thus the schedule should first of all be prepared on trial basis, should be tried any discrepencies in information sought, wording of question, their sequence etc. should be amended in the light of the experience thus gained.

Types of Questions

The different kind of questions that are asked in a schedule or questionnaire can be classified into the following types.

1. *Open end questions*—These questions generally relate to opinion sought about any particular problem or suggestions invited about it. Naturally answers to these questions are long and varied. There is no prior classification or grouping into which replies are likely to be received. There is a wide range of choice for the informant to give any reply. Not only the substance of the replies but also method of reporting may differ from person to person. Naturally open end questions present a great difficulty in tabulation. They are, however, used mostly in pilot studies to get an idea of the possible replies. When that has been known the replies are grouped into definite categories and included in the main schedule. Following are the examples of open end questions:

1. What, do you think, are the main causes of present indiscipline among the students ?
2. What suggestions do you offer to remove it.

2. *Structural Questions*— When answer to a question has been preconceived and classified into possible groups it is known as a structured question. Generally the answer to these questions may either be a number or some specific words. Thus the possible replies to structured questions are already known and they are grouped into various classes. The tabulation of a structured question is thus very easy. There is greater standardisation and objectivity in the replies. Here the method of reporting for the same answer does not differ and there is perfect homogeneity in reporting. Following are the illustrations of structured question:

1. What is your age?
2. Are you educated/or illiterate/semi-illiterate?
3. Are you married/bachelor/widow—widower/divorced.

3. *Dichotomous questions*— When reply to a question is given in form of one of the two alternatives the question is called dichotomous. Generally one of the answers is positive and the other negative, and the two combined form the whole range of answers. Dichotomous questions are very good in classifying and tabulating. There is no danger of any possible alternative being left out. An illustration of dichotomous question:

(a) Sex of the informant—male/female.

(b) Whether belongs to scheduled caste. Yes/no

4. *Multiple choice questions*—They are also known as *Cafeteria questions.* It is the opposite form of dichotomous questions. In these questions the reply is not confined to two alternatives only, buy may be one among a number of possible replies. A great care has to be taken to see that all the alternatives have been included. Generally a new group known as 'others' is included over and above the possible replies. Any omission of a group may seriously affect the nature of replies. In a study into the sources of community funds made by Prof. Young, he omitted to give 'endowment,' as a possible source. There was no column for 'other sources.' The result was that although endowment was one of main sources of income, it was not at all reported.

When the opinion about some matter is needed the serial arrangement of the alternatives also affects the replies. A care should be taken to avoid any bias being caused in this way. An illustration of the multiple choice question is given below:

1. What type of career do you propose to choice ?

(a) Business or Industry.

(b) Government Service.

(c) Private Service.

(d) Profession.

(e) Vocation.
(f) Any other (specify).

5. *Leading questions*—When reply to a question is suggested in a particular direction it is known as leading, suggestive or directive question. It is not necessary that reply to such a question may always be 'Yes' but the undecided cases are generally drawn towards it, thus creating a bias in the reply. Leading questions should be avoided as far as possible but when special emphasis has to be given to any particular aspect they may be included. Following is the illustration of a leading question.:

1. Don't you think that education in municipal primary schools makes the children ill mannered ?
2. Isn't it more beneficial for the whole family that women, instead of doing service outside, should look after their family and children.

6. *Ambiguous questions*—When the language of the question is such that it may be interpreted in more than one ways, it is called an ambiguous question. Ambiguity in a schedule is the greatest defect and care should be taken in wording the questions in such a way that clear cut idea may be conveyed through them. Ambiguity may be caused in the following ways:

1. When the language or construction of the sentence is defective.
   Whether you are educated or uneducated. Yes/no.
2. When some word or words having more than one interpretation are used. For example:
   What type of schooling did you have? 'Schooling' here may mean type of school attended or type of education received.
3. When reply to a question can not be clear cut and. more than one replies have an equal weight e.g. Are

you in favour of economic planning or state control? Here the two categories are not clear cut and overlap each other.

When such phrases or words are used which are of a technical nature and carry a different connotation in the technical sense. For example in study conducted by Fortune magazine of America two phrases "initiation fee" and "strict entrance requirements" were used. An enquiry afterwards revealed that 50% of the respondents had followed the meaning of two phrases incorrectly.

7. *Ranking item questions*—These questions are given to record the preference of the respondents. Like multiple choice questions they also contain a number of alternatives. The only difference between the two is that where as in case of the multiple choice question only one of the given answers is to be selected, in case of ranking item questions order of preference is to be given for all. In this case also due care should be taken in giving proper sequence to the various alternatives in the schedule, as the order given in the schedule, has great influence upon the respondents. An illustration of ranking question is given below:

1. What is your preference to following posts ?

(a) Director of a Company. ( )
(b) Indian Administrative Service. ( )
(c) Director of a research institute. ( )
(d) Professor of a first rate university. ( )
(e) A high court advocate of good fame. ( )
(f) A doctor. ( )

Lay-out of Schedule and General Form

The schedule must be attractive to look at. Attractiveness depends upon general form and layout of the schedule. The following factors must be taken into account for really perfect layout.

1. *Paper*—The paper to be used in the schedule should not be too rough or thin. A nice paper is not only decent to look at, but also makes writing upon it smoother and easier. The paper should be durable too, so that it may be capable of being kept in record for long time. Quality of paper also depends upon the amount of writing and erasing needed, and whether pencil or ink has to be used.

2. *Size of schedule*—Generally small size is preferable because it is handy. An unduly long paper is very inconvenient to handle and when folded several times, it easily wears out. Generally the size of schedule depends upon the number of question in it or the size of the tables that are to be filled. At any rate the size must conform to standard size cabinet drawer. The most popular size is "8½ × 11." Only one size should be used as far as practicable.

3. *Margin*—Margin of 3/4" on one side and nearly 1/5" or 1/6" on the other side should be left out. Margin not only gives a nice appearance to the schedule but also makes filing easy. Besides this, any notes if necessary can be written along the margin. If longer notes have to be written wider margin should be kept.

4. *Spacing*—Proper spacing is also necessary. The lines should not be very closely printed so as, to give a jumbled up look. Enough space should be left to demarcate one question from the other and one group from the other. If blank space has to be left for writing answers, the space left out should be according to the probable length of the answer.

5. *Printing*—The schedule may be printed or may be cyclo-styled. If printed, different types should be used for heading, sub-headings and questions.

6. *Use of pictures*—Sometimes pictures are also used along with the questions to make them more attractive. Thus for example if a question is put to find the respondents preference for various jobs, a picture of man indicating that job may be

given beside each category. This method however is more common in case of questionnaires.

Contents of Schedule

The complete schedule may be divided into three parts according to the nature of contents:

(1) Introductory part.
(2) Main schedule.
(3) Instructions to the interviewer or observers.

1. *Introductory part*—This part contains introductory information about the schedule, investigation and the respondent. This part is more or less common to all the schedules and given generally in the same form. Following types of information is generally contained in the introductory part:

1. Name and heading of the survey giving the name, of the conducting authority.
2. Serial or case number.
3. General information about the interview e.g. name address, age, sex, post held, education etc. The information of this column differs according to the nature of enquiry.
4. Place of interview.
5. Data and time of interview.

2. *Main schedule*—After this preliminary part, comes the main portion of the schedule. It is the most vital part and has to be prepared with great care. The schedule consists of questions as well as blank tables where information to be supplied by the interviewee has to be filled. Nature of questions to be given in this part has been discussed at length else where in this very chapter.

3. *Instructions to interviewers*—The schedule generally contains exhaustive instructions for the interviewers. Although

the interviewers are personally explained and even practically trained in the work, still instructions in writing are necessary. Sometimes these instructions instead of being given along with the schedule are supplied separately to field workers. Written instructions are very useful especially when the field worker is staying apart and the schedules have to be sent to him by post.

The instructions to the field workers should be very clear cut and exhaustive. They should contain meaning and explanation to various units and technical terms, the general method to be followed in filling the schedule and the way in which the interview is to be carried on. Changes may be made in this portion if any difficulties are experienced. Clarifications and amendments should be dispatched to the workers at once. At any rate, such changes as changing the meaning of any unit or technical term method or interview, including or deleting any part in the schedule should be avoided in the middle of the survey, as this may affect the comparability of the data.

Questions to be Avoided

Following types of questions should be avoided:

1. *Too long questions*—The questions should not be so lengthy that it may be difficult for the respondent to follow easily. If a ling question must be given it should be broken up into parts. If a very long question is given the respondent will forget the significance of the early part by the time he reaches the end of the question.

2. *Complex question*—The questions of complex nature should also not be given. Such questions are very difficult to understand and the respondents have generally been found to be in the habit of giving some reply to even to such questions as they do not follow, rather than not replying them at all.

3. *Personal questions*—Questions regarding personal life of a respondent should be avoided unless they form the chief subject matter of the enquiry. People are generally reluctant to disclose their personal matters regarding family life, marital or sex relations, diseases etc.

4. *Suspicious Questions*—Questions regarding income, character etc. generally cause suspicion in the minds of the people. If such questions are given at the top, the respondent may refuse interview. Otherwise also such questions are not well entertained. Therefore, they should be avoided unless they are absolutely necessary.

5. *Embarrassing questions*—Such questions as may put, the respondent in a difficult position should also be avoided. Thus for example, if the opinion of a government employee is sought about his own officers, he may find himself in a difficult position to express correct opinion. Such questions as — Are you satisfied with your present job. If not, why? — are of the same nature.

6. *Leading questions*—Suggestive type of questions should be avoided as they result in biased replies. Detailed discussion about leading questions has been given earlier in this chapter.

7. *Questions whose answers can be otherwise procured*—If the information can be elicited through other means, a direct question should always be avoided.

8. *Question beyond the ambit of subject matter*—Every single question should be pertinent to enquiry. No superfluous question should be included. Inclusion of even one superfluous question may result in a lot of expenditure on collection and tabulation.

9. *Questions likely to yield inaccurate response*—There are some questions, in which a correct reply is a remote possibility. Such questions should also be avoided unless there is some check to test their accuracy. Thus questions regarding social

status, health, character etc. are bound to receive an incorrect reply and should not commonly be asked.

10. *Questions on universally accepted norms*—Every society bears some universally accepted norms, formed according to their conception of morals or nature of culture. In such a case the answer is most obvious and no body can be expected to go against the universally accepted morals or norms. Such obvious questions should also be avoided.

Nature of Questions

No hard and fast rules can be given for selection of the nature of questions to be asked. It all depends upon the individual nature of study, types of respondents, quality of field workers and other means of verifying the information. The following points may, be used for general guidance:

1. The questions should be few, short and clearly worded, simple and easy to reply.

2. They should be within the informational scope of the respondent. Questions beyond ones capacity to answer should be avoided. Thus, for example, if we ask a question to a person regarding his 'diabetes' we may not get a correct reply.

3. Tabulation plan must be kept in mind while framing questions. We must know what would be the likely answers and how they shall be tabulated. Questions that are unfit for tabulation should be avoided.

4. Questions should have a direct bearing upon the problem. Superfluous questions should be avoided at all cost.

5. Indirect questions may be asked sometimes to get a correct reply. Thus in an interview of homeless men question was asked—Are you married? Later on it was changed to — Where is your wife? The number of married returned in the second question was much larger.

6. Questions facilitating cross checking may be given. Thus the checking of income may be done by question on expenditure and saving. The cross checking avoids any manipulation by the respondent.

7. The questions should be inter-related with each other so that the sequence may be maintained and a checking may also be possible.

8. Units or technical terms used in the schedule should be kept as far as possible the same as have been used in some previous enquiry, unless they are found to be unsuitable for the purpose. Similarity of units makes the comparative study possible.

9. More favourable and unbiased replies may be received in case of impersonal questions. In replying personal questions, howsoever simple, people are very cautious and generally give coloured replies. Blankenship once experimented with following two questions:

(a) Do you consider it feasible to balance the budget ?

(b) Is it desirable to balance the budget ?

More favourable replies were received for the second.

10. The questions should be so framed that there is minimum of writing work. This may be done in number of ways. One of the two alternatives may be cancelled. Check mark (✓) may be placed against the right answer if there are many. A cross (X) may be placed against the incorrect replies. Care should be taken to see that similar marks are used in all the schedules and clear cut instructions to this effect are given to the interviewers.

11. The question should be thorough and no place for any doubt should be allowed. Thus words like 'last year' or 'next year' should be avoided. Instead, the actual year should be used. In the same way such questions as — what is your age? are not correct. They should be what was your age on last birthday or any given date.

12. When questions seeking the degree of intensity of feeling or conviction are asked—why, what, when and how questions should also be included. They should be properly rated or ranked. Such schedules have been discussed in detail in the other chapters.

Questions Sequence

Proper sequence of questions is also necessary for a correct reply. No hard and fast rules can be given but following points may be found to be of some value.

1. Simple and uncontroversial questions should be given first. The general rule is to proceed from simple to the complex. If complex, or controversial questions are given at the top the respondent may refuse to give interview. According to Goode and Hatt, "It seems to be more difficult for an informant to break off an interview than to refuse to begin at all." Therefore beginning should always be made from questions that may be simple and there is no hesitation in replying them.

2. Attention catching questions may also be given in the beginning. They may arouse the interest of the respondent and the interview may have a smooth running.

3. Questions seeking the advice of the informants may be given earlier. They tend to satisfy the vanity of the respondent, and he may be more willing to lend his co-operation in filling the schedule.

4. All questions regarding one topic should be grouped at one place. If there is a clash between time sequence and subject matter sequence the latter should be given priority.

5. The different groups of questions should not be placed in such a way that no sequence or relationship be visible. Each question and each group should appear to be a necessary chain in the schedule and should not appear as scattered, stray cases.

6. There should be no sudden jumping from one topic to the other. The change from one topic to another should be very smooth. If the respondent does not get sufficient time for the change over, the replies may not be perfectly correct.

Language and Diction

A great precaution is necessary in wording the questions. Proper wording and proper language is absolutely essential. The words should be simple, clear and unambiguous. Following types of words be avoided as far as possible.

(1) *Technical terms*—Technical terms, departmental words, should not be used unless the enquiry is of a departmental nature or so technical, that terms have to be used. If such words are used it is better to give explanations to the difficult ones. Abbreviations should be avoided as far as possible.

(2) *Local or unusual words that are not commonly spoken*—If they must be used their meaning should be given in brackets.

(3) *Words carrying emotional connotation*—e.g Private, or public sector, socialism, Indian-foreign etc.

(4) *Subjective or qualitative words*—e.g. Often, seldom, rarely, always, good, very good, fair etc.

(5) *Ambiguous words*—Nebulous words having more than one meaning or words used both in general and technical sense.

Pilot Studies and Pretests

Pilot studies and pretests are necessary measures for framing a perfect schedule. A pilot study is undertaken before a schedule or questionnaire is drafted, a pretest is taken after it has been completed. Pilot study is the preliminary study of the universe in question to get an early idea about it. It may be undertaken without any hypothesis or with provisional hypothesis. If gives an idea of different variables involved, nature of the problem, possible difficulties in interviewing, kind of response likely to be available etc. It is on the basis of this information that the actual schedule or questionnaire is formed. If the sample selected for the pilot study is similar to the main sample a complete idea about the nature of the problem and the respondents will be available and the schedule drafted will be more perfect.

On completing the preparation the schedule it is tested once again to find if any discrepancies have been left out. It is known as pretest. According to Goode and Hatt—"No amount of thinking, however logical the brilliant insight, is likely to take place of careful empirical checking." Some of the errors are such as can be found out only when the schedule has been actually put into operation. The schedule might be too lengthy, questions may be ambiguous, or beyond the capacity of the respondents to answer, they may be offensive in nature so that respondents may refuse to answer them. The pretest study clearly brings to light any such defects. In the light of this experience the schedule is amended and the new schedule is put to test again. Thus only after it has been perfected after several tests and retests that the schedule is put finally into practice.

Following are the main criteria of a defective schedule:

(a) A large proportion of 'don't know answers.'
(b) A large number of people refusing interview.
(c) In case of questionnaire refusal to return it.
(d) Comments of interviewers or respondents.
(e) Defects of sampling—some part might have been left out altogether.
(f) Similar type of people giving different types of replies.
(g) Answers differing from the known answers.

If these discrepancies are noticed, their cause must be find and if it is due to any defect in the schedule, the same must be removed and the amended schedule, should be prepared.

Organisation of Interview through Schedules

In the first part of this chapter, we have discussed the basic principles for the construction of a schedule. Now we shall see how investigation is carried on with the help of schedule. After the schedule has been prepared, it may be utilised for observation or for interview. We shall here confine our discussion to interview alone and shall take up the use of schedule in observation at some later stage. The following steps are generally taken in organising interview through schedules:

1. Selection of interviewees.
2. Selection and training of field workers.
3. Method of carrying on interview.
4. Testing the validity of replies.
5. Editing the schedules.

Selection of Interviewees

After properly preparing the schedule the first thing to be done is to select the persons from whom the information is to be collected. This depends upon whether, the census or sampling method has to be used. If sampling method is to be used the sample has to be drawn. After the sample has been drawn the names and addresses of the persons to be contacted should be noted, so that they may be easily approached.

Selection and Training of Field Workers

If the number of persons to be contacted is very small, the investigator may himself conduct the work of the interviewing but generally the number is too large and the help of the field workers may be taken. A due care should be taken in selecting the right type of field workers. No hard and fast rules can be given but following are some of the qualities for an efficient field worker.

1. *Honesty*—The first essential quality of a field worker is honesty. If the field worker is dishonest he may be fill up

the whole schedule at his own place, after he has got preliminary information from the informant. As the schedule has to be filled by the field worker himself; there is no way to detect these dishonest practices except by test checking. But test checking can not be carried on any large scale, and the researcher has to depend upon the honesty and integrity of the field worker. It is more so when the field work is being carried on at long distance and the investigation is not personally present at the place of interview. The first precaution, therefore, necessary is that the field workers should be honest and sincere. Persons of doubtful integrity should never be taken in, even if they possess other requisite qualifications.

2. *Tactfulness*— The field worker should be very tactful. He must know how to deal with people. It must be known that the informants do not stand to gain in any way by spending their time and disclosing their own personel matters to an unknown person. The general tendency on the part of most of the informants is to avoid an interview if possible. All sorts of replies may be given "I am extremely busy at this time. Some guests have just arrived. Please come again after some time or I don't want to bother myself with all that nonsense etc." A clever field worker knows they are not the last replies. He must be able to know the weak point and bring the informat round by tactful means. Cases are not wanting when people who had given point blank refusal to be dragged into an interview became staunch supporters of the project, merely because of the tactful handling by the field workers. The field worker, therefore, has to act according to temperament of the interviewee and circumstances of the case. Only tactfulness is of any real help in dealing with such cases.

3. *Patience*—The field worker should have ample patience in him. He must be prepared to face people who are proud enough to refuse even to see him, or blunt enough to pass insulting remarks or talk in an offending tone. The field

worker as such times has to be extremely patient and forbearing. He must not lose his temper in the face of most provocative behaviour of the respondents. He must possess an unconquerable faith in the good sense of people and must believe in the principle that all such people can be made to co-operative if he pursues his work with great patience without losing his heart or temper.

4. *Smartness*—The interviewer should be smart, dynamic and active. While dull, lazy and slow witted person generally creates aversion in the minds of people. The first contact in case of direct interview with the interviewer, and the impression that the respondents forms about the nature or calibre of the research and the investigating body, is first of all through the interviewer. The schedule and the introductory letter one sees only afterwards, when he has agreed to see the interviewer. Smart youngmen with pleasing personality are always good field workers as it is always the pleasure to talk to such people. Besides the people will always hesitate in refusing interview to nicely dressed smart young man for the sake of courtesy if not for any other reason.

5. *Interest in research*— The field workers should have prompt zeal for research work. Although the field workers are mostly paid, the remuneration is generally not commensurate with the nature of work. The field worker has to face many novel situations in course of interview. Human beings differ in nature and temperament and the field worker has to handle them accordingly. He has to be careful not only for the fact that interview is granted, but also for the fact that the schedule is correctly replied. All this requires a direct interest of field worker in the research, an interest to find the truth behind the phenomena. The interest in research also keeps his morale high and he can successfully avoid any chance for dishonest practices. Interest in research however, does not means a prejudice or an interest in the particular result of the study.

6. *Unbiased and scientific outlook*—The field worker should possess purely scientific outlook. He should be free from any bias or prejudice Purely objective attitude is extremely difficult to achieve, but if the field worker is not deliberately interested in the outcome of the study he may be relied upon for the purpose of objectivity. The structured nature of schedule is an important check upon any bias being introduced by the field worker. But if he is strongly baised he may deliberately exercise his influence upon the interviewees to get the desired reply and thus create bias in the schedule.

7. *Vigilance*—The field worker should be very vigilant and alert. He is not only to see that the schedule has been filled and the interview taken. He should also see that it has been correctly filled. The field worker should always keep an eye over the expressions of the respondent. He must compare the answers with the observations. He should see whether the respondent is not simply befooling him and whether he is not giving a coloured or exaggerated account. Whenever in doubt he must put supplementary questions, to verify his statement by actual observation, or even verify the statement from those who know the respondent.

8. *Knowledge about the general nature of the class study*—The field worker should preferably possess the knowledge of the language, culture and customs of the class being studied. This will help him to approach the informants with greater familiarity and less resistance. He can exercise due care that his conduct is not offending in the nature, in the context of the informant's culture. Thus, for example, ladies of Hindu families do not tell the name of their husbands, and if the field worker insists upon it, the lady may feel offended, and even refuse to reply further questions. Besides, when the informant sees that the interviewer is completely ignorant about his (respondent's) culture he has the general temptation to exaggerate facts and tell lies with impunity.

9. *Training in methods of study*—Above all the field worker

must be trained in the method used in the conduct of investigation. Any lack of the qualities mentioned above can be made good by proper training. If training accompanied with experience it is all the better. In fact it is experience along that brings perfection in an interviewer. It is experience alone through which the field worker knows the general likes and dislikes of the peoples, the method of bringing them round when they refuse to oblige him by granting interview, their weak points, the delicate problems about which the respondents have as a class general tendency to tell lies. No amount of theoretical knowledge can compensate for the great quality of field experience.

It is very difficult to know whether field worker possesses all those desired qualities. Various methods of selection may be adopted. The respondents may be put to objective tests, they may be given a practical trial. Sometimes help of professional field workers is taken. In some of the advanced countries, there are institutes that provide experienced field workers on hire. In case of short surveys it is always more economical to hire them rather than train them.

Despite the field workers are experienced, some training has to be given to them regarding the particular project. This is generally done either through short time courses or simple conferences. In the preliminary conference all the field workers are called together. The importance and the purpose of study is explained to them. Then they are supplied with the schedule. Each and every question or table is read out, and thoroughly discussed. The clear meaning and significance of various terms used is also explained. The field workers are trained, how to fill up the forms. Sometimes code numbers or abreviations have to be used for different kinds of replies. If it is so they must be standardised and predetermined and thoroughly practised by the field workers. The field workers should also be explained the method of conducting the interview, how they are to approach the respondent, what line of action they are to adopt under different unfavourable circumstances. It is better if the field workers are told in advance the difficulties that they may have to face, so that they may be fully prepared and not be caught unawares. They must be told about the various types of querries likely to be made by the respondents before granting interview and also be told the answers that are to be given. In the end the field workers should be given practical training by model interviews. In the early stage the work of each field worker should be very closely watched and those who are found to be totally unfit for the job should be replaced.

Method of Carrying on Interview

This is the most important part of investigation. The questions to be dealt in this part are — How to approach the respondent to get a response, how to get correct replies and last of all how to end the interview. We shall here deal with each question one by one.

(a) *Approaching the respondent*—A correct approach is very essential. Sometimes when the respondent has given point blank refusal on principle, he makes it a prestige point to stick to it. The field worker should never allow such a situation to develop, and take due precaution in approaching the respondent. The interviewer should know the address correctly. It may be useful to get some preliminary knowledge about his nature, job, family etc. from other sources first. A proper time for interview is essential. If the respondent is in hurry he is very likely to refuse interview or give hurried half hearted replies. The leisure time should be chosen for the purpose. Evening and afternoon time has been found to be best in this respect. Generally the field worker has to approach directly with only the letter of introduction from the research body. An introduction from some influential person or friend of the respondent may be found to be helpful, but at times it has an adverse effect. The respondent may get scared that the interviewer is known to his friends and may leak out his personal information to him. He may thus be tempted to give manipulated replies. It has generally been found that we are more free to discuss our problems with totally aliens than with those who are known to us. This quality is technically known as 'stranger value.' How to call at the door is also a technical point which should be given due care. The first address must be impressive, dignified polite and appealing.

(b) *Getting response*—Getting response and making the respondent agreeable to interview is another major problem. Once the respondent has agreed to be interviewed, he is not likely to break off in the middle. At the very outset the field worker must know that people have a general apathy towards granting an interview and would look for the first excuse to avoid him. If the respondent has refused to permit an interview, the field worker should at once try to know the cause of it and hit at the very root of it. An interview may be refused because of the following reasons:

1. If the respondent is really busy and has no time to spare. In such a case the field worker should ask for a more convenient time to come.
2. The respondent simply wants to avoid the interview as he does not want to be bothered about it. If this is the cause the field worker should try to explain to him the importance of the study and how his own response is significant in the case.
3. The respondent is afraid to grant an interview. Probably it affects his boss, or party to which he belongs, or any other cause which he is likely to harm his interest. The field worker at such times must lay emphasis upon the secrecy that is maintained by research body and show to him the written pledge to this effect.
4. The respondent does not hold a high opinion about the outcome of such interviews in general, or has a poor opinion about the research body conducting it or the problem itself. The field worker should to explain

to him the importance of the problem and convince him regarding the status of the research body.

5. If the respondent is suspicious. He thinks that it is either from income tax department or C.I.D. or some other secret agency. At such times he may generally begin with questions—Who are you? Who told you my name? Have you interviewed the neighbour? etc. The field worker should try to remove his suspicion. The letter of authority, the letter head or seal of the research body is generally useful at such occasions.
6. The respondent is solitary-loving, unsocial or otherwise confined to his own family. Such a tendency is mostly found in case of newly married couples. The field worker at such times will try to create his interest in the subject of investigation.
7. The respondent is highly temperamental and thinks it below dignity to grant an interview to petty field workers. At such times either the investigator himself should see the respondent or get some letter of introduction from his friend, some influencial person.

The above are some of the most frequent or prominent reasons for refusing an interview. There may be many more such reasons. The duty of the field worker is to find out the exact cause of the refusal and try to convince him with the same point of view. The greatest difficulty in this respect is the fact that respondents simply refuse or avoid the interview, they do not give the reason straightaway. The field worker has to exercise his commonsense and experience to know the real cause from the nature of querries made by the respondent and act accordingly.

Checking the Schedule Returned by the Field Workers

When the field workers have returned the schedules, it is better to apply test checking to find that they have been properly filled. For this purpose a certain percentage of schedules is selected on random basis and the investigator himself interviews the respondents and tries to find any variation in replies. If a very significant difference is found on rechecking the whole lot must be rejected. The researcher must know the permissible limit of variation. If rechecking shows a slight variation, it does not necessarily mean invalidity of the previous schedule. The replies of a person, specially about his opinion and attitude are influenced by time factor also. A due allowance has to be given to these influences.

Rechecking should be done at an early date. The schedules should not be allowed to accumulate. They should be sent to the head quarter in convenient lots and atonce rechecked by the investigator. Early checking results in early detection of errors and location of persons responsible for the error. Besides, the influence of time factor is also not allowed to work upon the replies. If the scope of enquiry is very vast, several stages of rechecking may be planned and devised.

Getting a Correct Reply

The field worker should be vigilant to see that no false replies are given by the respondent. Much of the correctness depends upon the schedule itself and the nature of questions contained in it. The interviewer has no hold over it. But if he finds that the respondent has not understood the questions, he may read it out again with proper emphasis or even explain it to him. If he feels that respondent is trying to hide some fact or exaggerate it he must put supplementary questions and try to verify it.

Editing the Schedules

After the schedules have been received and rechecked, they have to be edited. Editing involves the following processes:

1. Checking the schedules;
2. Checking the entries;
3. Re-writing dirty and badly written schedules; and
4. Coding.

1. *Checking the entries*—The first step is to check the entries one by one. The editor must see that all the entries have been duly filled. If any column is left out an attempt should be made to know the cause. Some of the entries appear irrelevant or irregular at the very face. Wherever there are chances of cross checking the same must be applied. If different replies have been given by same types of persons, such answers should be carefully scrutinised. In case of any doubt the schedule should be refeerred back to the field worker. If the error has been caused by some slip and can be corrected in office the same must be done.

2. *Checking the schedules*—When filled up schedules have been returned, they are checked in the office to see that all of them have arrived. Division of cases on area basis or field worker basis is made and as the schedules from different areas or different field workers arrive, they are filed separately. A slip is generally placed at the top of the bundle giving information about (a) the total number of cases alloted in the area, (b) number of cases contacted (c) number of cases lost due to refusal, change of address, non-availability etc. If there has been any replacement of cases the same must also be mentioned in the slip. The slip is usually filled and signed by the field worker himself. If some of the cases have been rechecked, their number, names, differences noted etc. should be sent along with the bundle. The schedules are then compared with the names of cases in the sample and any discrepency is informed to the field worker.

3. *Dirty and badly written schedules*—In spite of the best precautions some of the schedules may be written in very dirty and illegible hand writing. They might have become mutilated due to unnecessary folding. Pencil might have been used for writing purpose. Field worker might have used his own abbreviations and forgotten to correct them afterwards. All such schedules are rewritten in clear hand writing. If some entry can not be followed properly, the same must be referred back to the enumerator concerned.

4. *Coding*—For the purpose of tabulation code numbers are generally given to various replies. Coding is essential for mechanical tabulation. For the purpose of coding the replies are first classified and a number is allotted to each class. Thus for example if a question is asked whether a person is married or unmarried there can be only four possible replies (1) married (2) unmarried (3) widow or widower (4) Divorced or separated. A number may be allotted for each answer. Thus by means of coding the qualitative answers are changed into specific numbers.

Sometimes code numbers are told to the field workers, and they may note down the code numbers in place of actual replies. But for the sake of accuracy it is better to codify them afterwards. After the schedules have been edited, they are ready for tabulation and analysis.

Merit of Interview through Schedules

The main merits of conducting an interview through schedules are as follows.

1. The field worker may recreate an atmosphere for proper response. He may start a disscussion, develop the interest of the respondent before showing the schedule. A right atmosphere is very helpful for getting corrected replies.

2. The schedule is filled by the field worker himself. He may follow short cut methods of recording and the interview may be finished much earlier. Besides, a tempo of discussion is maintained and the whole interview appears, to be one discussion rather than answering of stray questions. The respondent does not feel tired or bored. Supplementary questions may be put to enliven the whole discussion. Moreover, the difficulties of bad handwriting use of pencil etc., are also avoided as every schedule is filled by the interviewer.

3. The personal contact with the respondent enables the field worker to probe more deeply into the character, living

conditions and general life pattern of the respondent. These factors are very important to understand the background of any reply. A reply that may appear to be absolutely strange and uncalled for, may be found to be absolutely natural viewed from these backgrounds. An interview if properly conducted can supply much useful information over above the one called in the schedule, and may form basis of further enquiries on the subject.

4. The percentage of response is much higher than in case of mailed questionnaire. The field worker is personally present, and respondent generally finds it very difficult to refuse to grant him an interview. Thus all the cases excepting those who are strongly opposed or adamant not to reply can be contacted. If there is any mistake in the address, or the respondent has changed the address the same may be known and corrected. In case of a mailed questionnaire such a facility is absent.

5. The field worker is personally present to remove any doubt or suspicion regarding the nature of enquiry or meaning of any question or term used. The answers are therefore, not biased because of any mis-understanding. Moreover, the field worker is there to check that the answers are not absolutely exaggerated. He will verify them with what he has seen, put cross questions, consult the neighbours or those who know him in case of any grave doubt about the reply. Besides the respondent has to reply questions all atonce and gets no time for manipulating facts as in case of questionnaire. The answers of a schedule are generally more correct and representative than the questionnaire.

6. Personal contact may reveal any defect in the sampling. Some important cases might have been left out and can be known from the actual visit. Similarly defects of schedule can also be easily located. If some important questions or aspects of the problem have been left out in the schedule, the same can be located by direct contact, and discussion with

the respondent. That is why even in case of mailed questionnaire, the pilot study and pretest are conducted by direct interview method.

4. Finally, the schedule method provide an opportunity for human element to be present at the time of filling the schedule. This lifeless questionnaire, howsoever tactfully drafted, and attractively printed can be no match to the living field worker who is personally present to enliven the whole atmosphere with interesting discussion, act as an active counterpart to the interview, share his emotions and feelings and encourage him freely and frankly expressing his/her views.

Limitations

The method of schedules, in spite of its various advantages has limitations as mentioned below:

1. The presence of the field worker while on the one hand, encouraging the respondent to reply, may also prove a source of bias in the interview. At times the opinion of the respondent influenced by the field worker and he may reply not what he thinks to be correct but what he thinks the investigator wants. The field worker may actively take sides, and try to influence the response deliberately. If there is such loophole, the damage is irrepairable and cannot be prevented even with best precaution.

2. The method creates administrative problem too, particularly if the area to be covered is large and respondents are widely dispersed. An elaborate organisation has to be set up for training of the field workers, supervision of their work, rechecking of schedules etc. All this is not required in case of mailed questionnaire method.

3. It is a very costly affair. The cost per case is much higher in the method of schedules than in case of mailed questionnaire. A large number of field workers has to be engaged, and trained in the work of collection of data. Extra

staff is needed for the supervision of their work. Conveyance charges have to be paid to the field workers. All this entails a lot of expenditure and a researcher with limited financial means finds himself in difficulty to adopt this method.

We hope, the discussion on preceding pages will help the investigator conduct the research work smoothly in right direction. A seasoned researcher can make use of these besides his empirical knowledge of the field.

CHAPTER 8

Data Collection for Social Research: Nature & Purpose

By the data collection we mean to a purposive gathering of information relevant to the subject-matter of the study from the units under research. The method of collection of data depends mainly upon the nature, purpose and the scope of inquiry on one hand the availability of resources and time on the other. Statistical data may be classified into primary and secondary depending upon the nature of data and collection mode.

Primary and Secondary Data

Primary data are empirical observations gathered by the researcher or his associates for the first time for any research and used by them in the statistical analysis whereas secondary data are collected by others in the past and used by others. The difference between primary and secondary data is only of the degree of detachment with the original source. The data which are primary one time may be secondary at another. Once the primary data have been used, it loses its original character and becomes secondary. Such secondary data are mostly published in newspapers, periodicals and journals.

Selection of Primary and Secondary Data

The choice between primary and secondary data mainly depends upon the nature, objectives and scope of inquiry, availability of time and money, degree of accuracy desired and the status of the researcher. The primary data are more reliable on the face, but the secondary data can be relied only by examining the source from which they have been obtained, their true significance, incompleteness and method of collection. Sometimes in a certain research both primary and secondary data are used as supplement to each other. It may be pointed out that today in a large number of statistical inquiries secondary data are generally used because of availability of fairly reliable published data on a large number of diverse fields. In fact, primary data are collected only if there do not exist any secondary data suited to the research under study.

The following points are noteworthy for the preference of primary source in comparison to the secondary source:

(i) The primary source gives data in greater details compared to secondary source. The secondary source often omits part of the information.

(ii) In the secondary source, there is a possibility of mistakes due to errors in transcription made then the figures were copied from the primary source.

(iii) The primary source includes definitions of terms and units used. It is essential that the researchs understand the meaning of units in which data are recorded.

(iv) The primary source also includes a copy of the schedule used in data collection together with the prescription of the procedure used in selecting the sample and the size of the sample.

(v) The availability of time at the disposal of researchs also affect the choice of the method to be adopted in the collection of data. If the data are needed immediately. We have to depend upon the secondary source. On the other hand, if the time is sufficient, it is recommended to use primary method of data collection because primary data are more accurate and reliable compared to secondary data.

(vi) The objective and the scope of the enquiry also determine the method to be adopted in the collection of data. The selected method must suit the objective and the scope of the enquiry.

(vii) The availability of finance also influences the method to be adopted in the collection of data. If the data collecting authority has vast financial resources at its disposal, it is better to adopt primary method. On the contrary, if the data collecting agency has less financial resources, secondary source should be adopted even though the secondary data are not as reliable as primary data. For example, research scholars mostly depend upon secondary data due to shortage of money.

(viii) The availability of trained researchs also affect the choice of the method to be employed in data collection. If trained researcher are available, primary method should be adopted for the collection of data. In case of non-availability of trained researchers, it is recommended to adopt secondary method of data collection.

Prerequisite to Data Collection

The collection of data is the first step for any statistical research. But in a scientifically prepared (efficient and well planned) statistical enquiry, the collection of data is by no means the first step. Before we embark upon the collection of data for a given statistical enquiry, it is imperative to examine carefully the following points.

Scope and Objectives of the Enquiry

The foremost step in organising any statistical enquiry is to define in clear and concrete terms the objectives of the enquiry. This is very essential for determining the nature of the statistics (data) to be collected and also the statistical techniques to be employed for the analysis of the data.

The objectives of the enquiry would be help in eliminating the collection of irrelevant information which is never used subsequently and also reflect upon the uses to which such information can be put. In the absence of the purpose of the enquiry being explicity specified, we are bound to collect irrelevant information and also omit some important information which will ultimately lead to fallacious conclusions and wastage of resources.

Further, the scope of the enquiry will also have a great bearing upon the data to be collected and also the techniques to be used for its collection and analysis. Scope of the enquiry relates to the coverage with respect to the type of information, subject-matter and geographical area. For instance, if we want to study the cost of living index numbers, it must be specified if they relate to a particular city or state or whole of India.

Statistical Units to be Used

A well defined and identifiable object or a group of objects with which the measurements of counts in any statistical research are associated is called as statistical unit. For example, in a socio-economic survey the unit may be an individual person, family, a household or a block of locality. A very important step before the collection of data begins is to define clearly the statistical units on which the data are to be collected. In a number of situations the units are conventionally fixed like the physical units of measurement such as metres, kilometers, quintals, hours, days, week, etc. which are well defined and do not need any elaboration or explanation. However, in many statistical researchs, particularly relating to socio-economic studies arbitrary units are used which must be clearly defined. This is imperative since in the absence of a clear cut and precise definition of the statistical units, serious errors in the data collection may be committed in the sense that we may collect irrelevant data on the items, which should have, in fact, been excluded and ommit data on certain items which should have been included. This will ultimately lead to fallacious conclusions.

Sources of Information

Once the scope and the purpose of the enquiry have been defined, the next problem arises how the data are to be collected? There are two methods which may be employed for the collection of data:

(i) An original enquiry may be conducted for data collection.

(ii) Data collected by some other agency may be used.

When an original enquiry is conducted for the collection of data, it is named primary method and the collected data are called primary data. On the other hand, when data collected by some other agency are employed for the analysis of the problem at hand, it is called secondary method and the collected data are called secondary data.

Now the question crops up, which type of data—primary or secondary—should be employed for studying the behaviour of variables? This decision cannot be undertaken independently but depends upon the purpose and scope of the enquiry. In most of the enquiries relating to current problems, it is recommended to use primary data than secondary data. Whenever secondary data are to be used, it is always necessary to examine the following questions:

— Who collected the data?
— How the data were collected?
— Was the correct method used for the data collections?
— Whether the collected data are sufficient for the present enquiry or not.
— Whether the purpose and the scope of the post enquiry were the same as that of the present enquiry.

Types of Enquiry

Statistical enquiries may broadly be classified under for headings which are discussed below:

— *Open or Confidential*: A statistical enquiry is termed open when its findings are made public through publications. On the contrary, when findings of an enquiry are kept secret it is called confidential.

— *Original or Repetitive*: An enquiry, when is conducted for the first time, is called original. On the other hand, an enquiry which is conducted in continuation is called repetitive.

— *Official or Non-official*: An enquiry which is conducted on behalf of the government is named official enquiry whereas an enquiry conducted by a private authority or an institution is called non-official.

— *Census or Sample*: A census type enquiry is one in which information is collected about each and every individual item in the population whereas in a sample enquiry, only a few selected items in the population are studied. On the basis of information gathered from these items, conclusions are drawn about the nature of the population.

Now the question crops up which type of enquiry is to be used in the collection of data. Here there was no hard and fast rules which may be laid down for selecting the type of enquiry.

Requirements of a Statistical Unit

The following are the main requirements which a statistical unit should possess:

It must be Specific and Unmistakable

A statistical unit employed in the collection of data must be specific and unmistakable. Such a unit will be interpreted in the same sense by different persons and the collected data could be homogeneous in nature. If the unit is ill-defined, different persons would interpret it in different fashions to suit their own way of thinking and the collected data would be heterogenous in nature unfit for comparison.

It should be Stable

The second requirements of a good statistical unit is stability. If there are continuous changes in the definition of unit, the data collected at different times would become unfit for comparison. The utility of such data is lost. Therefore, the unit must be stable for meaningful comparison.

It should be Homogeneous

A statistical unit employed in the collection of data must be homogeneous throughout the enquiry. It must not imply different characteristics at different times and at different places. If a single unit is not applicable to all cases under study then this problem can be solved by sub-dividing data in uniform groups.

It must be Appropriate to Enquiry and Capable of Correct Ascertainment

The statistical unit selected for the collection of data should be appropriate to the enquiry and capable of correct ascertainment. For example, when compiling labour statistics, it is necessary to select the unit appropriate to the information required, e.g., workers engaged directly on production, those employed in indirect factory services those in administrative office or those in sales department.

Types of Statistical Units

There are two types of statistical units:

Units of Collection

Such units are concerned with the collection of data. They take the form of counts and measurements. Examples of units of measurement are production of wheat in quintals, height in inches or weight in kilograms and examples of units of counting are the number of persons in a family, number of rooms in a house or number of houses.

Units of collection may further be divided into two categories, namely:

(i) *Simple Unit:* A simple is one which describe a single determining characteristic such as wage, weight ton yard, etc., such units are not difficult to define and are in common use. But care must be taken in interpreting some of them. For example a wage may be defined as money wage or kind wage.

(ii) *Composite Unit:* A composite unit is one which is formed by the addition of some qualifying condition to a simple unit. For example, electric power is measured in units of kilowatt-hours while railway transport is expressed in ton-miles and ton-miles are equal to the number of tons multiplied by the number of miles carried. Other examples of composite units are educated unemployed, factory building man-hours or passenger miles.

Units of Analysis

Statistical data are collected for analysing the behaviour of the variable under study. Therefore, units of analysis are those with which statistical data are analysed and interpreted. These units are employed for making comparisons between two or more series or variables. Suppose we are told that the sales of firm 'A' has increased by 8% and of firm 'B' by 15% in 1985 we can easily conclude that firm 'B' made more progress than firm 'A'.

Method of Data Collection

The problem does not arise if secondary data are to be used. However, if primary data are to be collected a decision has to be taken whether (i) census method, or (ii) samples technique, is to be used for data collection. In the census method, we resort to 100% inspection of the population and enumerate each and every unit of the population. In the sample technique we inspect or study only a selected representative and adequate fraction (finite subset) of the population and after analysing the results of the sample data we draw conclusions about the characteristics of the population. In some situations such as population being infinite or very large, census method fails. Moreover, it is not practicable, if the enumeration or testing of the units (object) is destructive, e.g., for testing the breaking strength of chalk, testing the life of electric bulbs or tubes, testing of crackers and explosive etc. Even if practicable, it may not be feasible from considerations of time and money. Thus, a choice between the sample method and census method is to be made depending upon the objectives and scope of the survey, the limitations of resources in terms of time, money, manpower, etc. and the degree of accuracy desired. In case of sample method the size of the sample and the technique of sampling like simple random sampling, stratified random sampling, systematic sampling, etc. are to be decided.

Degree of Accuracy

The degree of accuracy which is desired must be decided in advance because the nature and quantum of data to be collected depend upon the desired degree of accuracy. As statistics deals with averages, so absolute degree of accuracy is not possible in statistical studies. Only reasonable degree if accuracy must be aimed at. The degree of accuracy which is to be achieved depends upon the purpose, the scope measuring rods and the attitude of the researchers and the informants. For example, while estimating the per-acre yield of wheat, it hardly makes any difference if one or two kilometers are ignored. On the other hand while measuring the height of a student we cannot afford to ignore even a centimeter. Thus in statistical studies a reasonable degree of accuracy may be sufficient because absolute accuracy is unattainable.

Methods of Collecting Primary Data

When the preliminary stages relating to a statistical inquiry have been satisfactorily arranged and the sources of data are listed, the next stage is the actual collection of the information. The following methods of collecting data may be distinguished:

— Direct personal interviews,
— Indirect personal interviews,
— Information received from correspondents,
— Mailed Questionnaire—to be filled in by the informations, and
— Questionnaires in-charge of enumerators.

Direct Personal Interviews

Under this method, data are collected by the researcher personality by asking questions pertaining to the enquiry from persons from whom the information is to be obtained (known as informants). Thus, if a person wants to study the spending habits of the students of a university he may contact and interview students personally and collect the desired information. If an inquiry is to be conducted into the family budgets and living conditions of workers of a factory, the researcher may interview the workers and collect the information necessary for his research. As the researcher is present on the spot for conducting the enquiry, the data collected by him would be first hand and original in character.

Merits: Following are the advantages of Direct Personal Interview method:

— As the researcher approaches the informants personally the latter would part with the information without much hesitation.
— The results obtained by this method are generally accurate and reliable as the enquiry is intensive and is conducted personally. The researcher can remove the doubts of the informant about certain questions. Also if the researcher has any doubt about the answer to a question, he can get it removed from the informants by asking the question again.
— The interviewer establishes personal contact and can twist the questions keeping in mind the informant's reactions.

— The language of communication can be adopted according to the educational level of the informant.

— Any other additional information about the personal characteristics of the informants may be collected, which will provide a background at the time of interpretation of data.

Limitations: Some limitations of this method are:

— Its nature limits its scope. It cannot be extensive in its scope. If the number of persons to be interviewed is large and they are spread over a wide area, this method cannot be useful as it requires the personal attention of the researcher. Thus such personal researchs are generally local-restricted to one town or area, e.g., inquiry into the family budgets and living conditions of factory workers.

— If the inquiry is a bigger one, then it cannot be completed within a reasonable time.

— The subjective factor is generally involved either consciously or unconsciously.

— The interviewers have to be thoroughly trained and supervised, otherwise results obtained may not be accurate and reliable.

Suitability: On account of physical and financial limitations this method is suitable when the field of enquiry is small.

Indirect Personal Interviews

Under this method facts are collected by interviewing persons who are directly or indirectly concerned with the subject-matter of the inquiry. For instance, Shah Commission has been appointed by the Government of India to enquire into the excesses during the period of Emergency. It may be distinguished from the first method in which information is collected directly from the persons who are involved in the inquiry. In case of indirect personal observation, information is collected from persons who are in possession of such information. The persons are known as witnesses or informants.

This method is generally used in those cases where the information to be obtained is of a complex nature, the area to be covered is vast or the informants are reluctant to respond if approached directly. For example, in an inquiry regarding addiction to alcoholic drinks, addicts may not be inclined to respond. In such a situation, the researcher has to approach their friends, neighbours, relatives, employers or dealers of liquor. Similarly, if an accident has taken place, the cause of accident can be found out by contacting persons who are present there or are living in that area. These witnesses or informants are invited to give evidence before the interviewers, who keep with themselves a list of carefully drafted questions pertaining to the object of enquiry-drinking habits or cause of accident. This method is generally adopted by enquiry committees or commissions appointed by the Government.

Though this method is very popular in practice, but certain precautions should be observed by the collecting agency otherwise the information obtained may not be reliable. These precautions are:

— It should be ascertained that the witnesses really possess the knowledge or information.

— It should be ascertained that they are not prejudiced in favour of or against a particular viewpoint. Thus does allowance should be given for their optimism and pessimism.

— Also, the interviewers should not be subjective in their approach. They may collect only such information which go to show results according to their whims. They should also understand the psychological and instinctive reactions of the persons whom they have insisted for interview.

Suitability: This method is suitable in the following cases:

— Direct sources do not exist, or cannot be relied upon, or would not be inclined to respond to give information.

— The enquiry is extensive.

Information from Correspondents

Under this method, the researcher appoints local agents or correspondents in different parts of the field of inquiry. They will be submitting their reports periodically to the central office, where the data will be processed. This method is generally adopted by newspapers and periodicals which require informations in different fields regularly. This method is also adopted by various departments of the governments in those cases where regular informations is to be collected from a wide area. Estimates of agricultural crops may be periodically furnished to the Government by village school teachers. Prices of different commodities entering into the construction of the wholesale price index numbers may be regularly collected by correspondents appointed in different areas and forwarded to the Government.

This method is comparatively cheap and also gives rough and approximate results promptly and easily. However personal bias of the correspondents may enter the reports and to that extent the accuracy of the information may be affected.

Suitability: This method is suitable in those cases where the information is to be obtained at regular intervals from a wide area and only rough and approximate estimates are required.

Mailed Questionnaire—To be Filled in by the Respondent

The collection of data through questionnaire is one of the most popular methods used these days. A questionnaire contains many questions pertaining to the field of inquiry and provides space for answers. It may be defined as an instrument for collecting information from a number of persons, supposed to possess it by making them record their replies to a number of questions. It is sent to the informant by post. The informant sends back the questionnaire duly filled in within the stipulated time mentioned in the covering latter sent with the questionnaire.

Merits: With the help of this method an extensive field may be surveyed and information elicited from persons living over a wide geographical area.

— This method of collecting information is very economical, as it involves the cost of printing the questionnaire and sending them to the informants.

— The information obtained by this method is also of good quality provided certain safeguards are observed which shall be explained a little later.

Limitations: This method presumes that the informants are literate and understand the language of the questionnaire. This presumption obviously limits the scope of this method to certain researchs only.

— A large part of the sample taken may not answer the questionnaire. Only 10% or 15% of the informants chosen may respond to the questionnaire, in which case the results obtained cannot be said to be reliable. The informants do not appreciate the purpose of enquiry and are indifferent to the public service they would be rendering by providing the information. Thus many questionnaires find themselves in waste paper baskets. Also, the results of inquiry will get vitiated by the response of only those who are interested in the study and not by those who are not interested.

— It is not easy to break through the pride and prejudices of informants; to make them communicate facts and opinions without distorting or colouring them. Thus the answers given may be incorrect, either because some of the questions contained in the questionnaire have not been properly understood by them or due to association of ideas, their exact connotation has been missed.

Certain Safeguards for Making the Method of Collection of Data by Questionnaire Method a Success

— The questionnaire should be pre-tested in a limited field to find out if the questions are proper and will be answered in the way desired.

— The need of the study should be clearly explained in the covering letter to the informants.

— A definite assurance should be given to the informants that their information would be kept secret and confidential.

— The questionnaire should be carefully framed. This will be explained a little later.

— Prepaid postage stamps should be affixed.

— A proper scheme should be devised for selecting individuals who would be approached to fill up the questionnaires.

— Follow-up letters may be written, if necessary.

— The questionnaires returned duly filled it should be scrutinise in order to detect any apparent inconsistency in them.

Suitability: If the above safeguards are provided, this method of collecting data would work effectively in case where informants are literate and are spread over a vast area.

Questionnaires In-charge of Enumerators

Sometimes the questionnaire is filled by the enumerator or the interviewer in which case it is known as *schedule.* In the case of a schedule, the enumerator fills the answers to the questions asked by him. The answers are given by the informant but they are written in the schedule by the enumerator in his own handwriting. This eliminates to a large extent the problem of non-response present in the case of mailed questionnaire method.

Merits:

- It can be adopted even in those cases where informants are illiterate.
- This method eliminates to a great extent the problem of non-response.
- The enumerators can explain the significance of the inquiry and the questions in the questionnaire personally to the informants and thus ensuring collection of accurate and reliable information.

Limitations:

- The enumerator might be a biased one and may not enter the answers given by the respondents truthfully. He may twist or suppress the information provided by the informant.
- Where there are many enumerators, they may interpret various terms in the questionnaire according to their own understanding of the terms. The interpretation might be quite unintentional.

To the extent mentioned above the information supplied may be either inaccurate or inadequate or not comparable.

- The bias may arise due to the state of mind of the informant or the environment in which he is placed.
- This method is somewhat costly and time-consuming since it requires a large number of enumerators who are paid persons.
- In the light of above, the success of the method depends largely on the training imparted to the enumerators as regards the significance of the enquiry and the terms used in the questionnaire.

Suitability: This method is most suitable where finance and trained enumerators are available to cover a wide field and where some significance is attached to the accuracy of the results obtained.

Questionnaire Construction and Design

The need for primary data require that a questionnaire be developed. Developing a suitable questionnaire is the most challenging aspect of research. The researcher must have some insight into the process of human communication and thinking and must be intelligent enough to anticipate the type of responses he may get in reply to certain questions.

The personal interview and mail or telephone surveys are common methods of contacting potential respondent to gather information related to the matter under research. Whatever the method employed questions are asked directly or indirectly.

A questionnaire is a format containing a list of questions sequentially ordered to obtain information relevant to the objectives of the study. A questionnaire is not only a list of questions used to obtain responses. It is specifically intended to obtain particular kinds of data. It should be designed, therefore, according to set specifications and with specific goals in mind. A questionnaire cannot be judged as good or bad, efficient or inefficient unless the job it was intended to accomplish is known. It is essential, then, to look at the development of a questionnaire as a whole rather than the mere wording of any one particular question.

Developing a questionnaire requires a certain amount of technical knowledge. During the early stages of research, the goals may undergo a number of subtle changes as the developer achieves greater clarity about them.

When developing a questionnaire, the researcher must decide what to ask potential respondents. Therefore, prior to questionnaire development, the researcher must make an outline of the several possible aspects of his research topic. At this stage, the researcher should write down every area in which additional facts would be helpful in the proposed research. Personal biases should be recognised but personal distortion should not be allowed to corrode the data-gathering process.

Before writing the questionnaire, the researcher must decide:

— the method of data collection.
— procedure to be followed in approaching the respondent,
— the order of sequence of questions within the framework of the questionnaire,
— direct verses indirect questions, and
— structured verses unstructured questions.

Information can be gathered from potential respondents by:

When information is gathered by personal interview or mailing the questionnaire, the respondent can read the questions and record answers without an interviewer's help, such a questionnaire is called a 'self administered' questionnaire.

Types of Questionnaire

It is possible to classify questionnaire studies on a variety of bases. Three such bases which are of importance are: (i) the degree to which the questionnaire is formalized or (i) structured; (ii) the disguise or lack of disguise of the objective of the questionnaire; and (iii) the communication method used.

Using the first two bases of classification, four types of studies can be distinguished:

(i) Structured Non-disguised

Most questionnaire studies made in marketing research are of the first type they are structured and are not disguised. Collection of data in a structured interview of this type has definite advantages in marketing research. By reducing the chance for interviewers to influence results through different phrasings of questions and even different questions, and through different judgments of answer and what to record, the structured questionnaire produces more reliable results.

Data obtained in structured, non-disguised studies are easier to tabulate and interpret than data gathered in other ways. Answers to former questions of clear purpose can be counted and their apparent meaning determined in a more objective fashion than is true for data obtained by other methods. Structured non-disguised studies can be handled by telephone, mail or personal interview.

Such studies tend to be limited to the collection of factual information or opinions. They are subject to the three limitations of the questionnaire method. Respondents may be unable to furnish the information desired, they may be unwilling to furnish it or the questioning process may tend to stimulate incorrect or misleading answers.

(ii) Non-Structured, Non-disguised Questioning

More than anything else, marketers want to know why people buy or do not buy their products. Direct questions dealing with motives rarely elicit useful answers. Instead of approaching respondents with a fixed list of questions, the interviewer attempts to get respondents to talk freely about the subject of interest. By doing so, the interviewer hopes to put respondents at case and to encourage them to express any ideas which they have on the subject. If some idea of interest is passed over too quickly, the interviewer may seek more information by probing. "Although, no formal questionnaire is used in interviewing of this type, the interviewer has an outline in mind. The objectives of these interviewers is to get below the respondents surface reasons for particular marketing decisions and to find the underlying or basic motives. This procedure is often called 'depth interviewing' for this reason".

This type of questioning secures more information from the respondents who is not kept in the strait jacket of a set list of questions. This flexibility on part of the interviewer is a major advantage of the method, but it is also a major weakness. Since each interviewer handles each interview differently, it is difficult to compare results. Average and percentage cannot be compared with validity.

Depth interviewers take longer than the typical structured interviewers. Many of them last for an hour or more. This creates two problems. One is cost as high period interviewers spend along time on each interview and thus lead to high total cost. As a result most studies using depth interviews are limited to very small samples.

A final and major disadvantage is the difficulty and cost of interpretation. Skilled psychologists must be used to interpret the results.

(iii) Non-Structured, Disguised Questioning

Many people are either unwilling or unable to give accurate reports as to their own attitudes and motivation. To overcome this difficulty, clinical psychologists have developed disguised methods of gathering such data. Disguised methods are designed so that the respondents do not know what the objective of the study is. Such disguised methods may also be unstructured. Projective techniques are an example of this type.

The theory of projectives techniques is that all individuals, in describing a situation, interpret that situation to a degree. The description given reflects a certain amount of the individual giving it. Thus, when individuals describe a situation, they are actually describing their interpretation of the situation.

Various projective techniques are used but the most common are word association, sentence compilation and story telling.

Since projective techniques are unstructured interpretation is very subjective, hence it is subject to the criticism that it reflects the interpreter as much as the respondent. Cost, time and difficulty in securing competent field workers are some of the other problems of projective techniques.

The big advantage of projective technique lies in their ability to uncover subconscious and specially unacceptable attitudes and motives. Moreover, there is greater standardization of the stimuli given to the respondent. Results are more comparable and less subject to bias as all respondents can be given exactly the same stimuli in projective tests.

(iv) Structured, Disguised Questioning

Questioning of the structured, disguised type has the advantage of disguise which are pointed out in the above points, primarily that respondents do not know what is being measured and hence are not biased in their answers. The advantage of structure lie in the reduction of interviewer and interpreter bias, in quicker and less costly interviewing and in easier tabulation of results.

Some structured, disguised tests of attitudes are based on the theory that individuals knowledge, perception and memory are conditioned by their attitudes.

Similarly, it is theorized that if respondents are asked questions to which they do not know answers, they will tend to guess in the direction of their own attitudes.

Data collected by structured, disguised techniques on attitudes towards instant coffee were compared with the similar data collected by non-structured, disguised techniques as described above. Although the samples in the two studies were not directly comparable, the results obtained with the simple structured, disguised questionnaire were similar in nature to those obtained by the non-structured approach. The structured study, however, benefited from having the prior data as a guide to the study design.

Developing A Good Questionnaire

A good questionnaire is one that helps, the researcher to obtain data related to the objectives of the study. The topic areas to be covered or the content of the questionnaire value out of what the researcher wants to accomplish from the proposed project. The types of questions or items to be included in the questionnaire and the format depend to a large extent on the types of data sought and the questionnaire design concepts and alternatives.

The researcher cannot develop a good questionnaire simply by increasing down what he thinks will provide him the type of data for which he is looking. Various steps are involved in developing a questionnaire that will provide the researcher with needed data. These steps are:

(i) Determining Questionnaire Contents

In determining the contents of the questionnaire, the researcher should consider the problem he wants to research the objectives or the hypotheses to be tested. Once these are specific and clear, the researcher should determine the contents of the questionnaire. To do this, he should review literature or previous studies related to the proposed project. This review of literature helps the researcher to discover the types of questionnaires or data collection procedures that others used under similar conditions. The contents covered by previous researchers may be usable in the proposed research product, or they may stimulate the researcher's thinking toward other areas to be included in the questionnaire to be developed.

At the beginning of the session, the researcher should make it clear that the purpose of the session is to generate possible content areas to be covered in the questionnaires that will be developed for collecting the needed data. The researcher should remind participants, as the discussion progresses that all suggestions are welcome however useless or silly they may seem to be at that time. Because the main purpose of a brainstorming session is idea generation, the researcher should make every effort to encourage each participants to build upon others, ideas in order to develop an extensive list of possible areas to be included in the questionnaire content. After a list is developed, the researcher should use his discretion and select only those content areas which he believes should be included in the questionnaire.

(ii) Developing Items to be Used

Once the researcher decides upon the content areas for the questionnaire, the next stop is to develop items with which to obtain data related to the content areas. The items can be questions or statements. They can be in the form of (a) structured or non-structured question, (b) rank-ordered questions, (c) rating scales, and (d) attitude scales, seldom are all these types put in any one questionnaire. It is not uncommon, however, to have a combination of one or more types in a single questionnaire.

The types of questions or items in a given study depends upon the objective of the study. A researcher should select only the type of items or questions that will best serve the purpose of the study.

Once the researcher has selected the types of items he should develop items to meet the needs of questionnaire content. The researcher should use his discretion and incorporate in the questionnaire sufficient items to accomplish the purpose of the study. Any item or question the researcher considers superfluous and not related to the objectives of the study should not be included.

(iii) Preparing the First Draft

Based on decisions made on items to be included in the questionnaire, the researcher do not develops the initial draft. This phase uses a trial and error approach with regard to the sequencing or arranging of items or questions and reviewing and revising until the researcher feels that the items are appropriate.

Sequencing items in a proper order is necessary because the questions included in the questionnaire, should be organised into logical groups. Grouping can be made on the basis of questionnaire content or on type of format of the items. Each section in every item or question must be reviewed to determine the type of instructions that should be given to the interviewers to facilitate easy and accurate completion of the questionnaire.

At this stage, the researcher also should decide on the format and layout of the questionnaire. In dealing with format, the researcher should pay attention to the title of the questionnaire, the margins, spacing, emphasis of key points or comments of the questionnaire and the overall length.

Thus, evaluation of the first draft involves analysis of overall format and layout of the questionnaire as well as the details of items included. Evaluation of initial draft may necessitate changes.

(iv) Pre-Testing

The revised draft should be tested before data are collected. The revised questionnaire should be pre-tested to determine how well it serves the purpose of obtaining needed data. Pre-testing to be done by administrating the questionnaire to a small but representative sample of potential respondents under conditions that are identical in all respects to those under which the final questionnaire will be administered.

Before revising the pre-tested questionnaire, the researcher should evaluate responses, comments and suggestions to determine how the questionnaire or the procedure for administering the questionnaire can be improved. Thus, pre-testing step serves as a vehicle for evaluating the usefulness of the questionnaire in obtaining the type of data sought for successful competition of the proposed study. While evaluating responses, comments and suggestions the researcher should remain open-minded and recognise any short-comings of the test questionnaire.

(v) Revising and Writing the Final Questionnaire

How much and to what extent a questionnaire subjected to pretest should be revised is primarily at the researcher's discretion or judgment. If a substantial number of respondents in the sample finds it difficult to understand an item, it should be revised.

Organization of the testing procedure and control are essential to reap the full benefits of pre-testing and arrive at a questionnaire which will accomplish the objectives of the study. After the test questionnaire is revised, the researcher should prepare the final questionnaire. In preparing, the final questionnaire, the researcher must take into account every aspect of the criticism of the initial draft and the results of pretesting.

Secondary Data

According to W.A. Neiswanger, "A primary source is a publication in which the data are published by some authority which has gathered and analysed them. A secondary source is a publication reporting data which has been gathered by other authorities and for which others are responsible." In simple words secondary data is one which is collected by some earlier agency but is used and analysed and any other for its own use. Data which are primary at one time may be secondary at another. Once the primary data have been used, it loses its significance, original character and becomes secondary. Secondary data are more popular in modern surveys since they are easily available, time-saving and economical.

SOURCES OF SECONDARY DATA

The chief sources of secondary data may be broadly classified into the following two groups: published sources & unpublished sources.

Published Sources

There are a number of national (government, semi-government and private) organisations and also international agencies which collect statistical data relating to business, trade, labour, prices, consumption, production, industries, agriculture, income, currency and exchange, health, population and a number of socio-economic phenomena and publish their findings in statistical reports on a regular basis (monthly, quarterly, annually, adhoc). These publications of the various organisation serve as a very veritable source of secondary data.

(i) *Official Publications of Central Government:* The following are various government organisations along with the year of their establishment [given in bracket ( )] which collect, compile and publish statistical data on a number of topics of current interest-prices, wages, population, production and consumption, labour, trade, army, etc.

- India (a Reference Annual) published by Ministry of Information and Broadcasting, Govt. of India.
- Office of the Registrar General and Census Commissioner of India, New Delhi (1949). In India census has been carried out every ten years since 1881. Prior to the establishment of this organisation, the census was conducted by a temporary cell in the Ministry of Home Affairs.
- Directorate-General of Commercial Intelligence and

Statistics, Ministry of Commerce (1895).

— Labour Bureau, Ministry of Labour (1946).
— Directorate of Economics and Statistics, Ministry of Agriculture and Irrigation (1948).
— The Indian Army Statistical Organisation (I.A.S.O.), Ministry of Defence (1947).
— National Sample Survey Organisation (N.S.S.O.), Department of Statistics, Ministry of Planning (1950). National Sample Survey (N.S.S.) was set up in 1950 in Ministry of Finance. In 1957, N.S.S. was transferred to the Cabinet Secretariat and named National Sample Survey Organisation (N.S.S.O.).
— Central Statistical Organisation (C.S.O.). Department of Statistics, Ministry of Planning (1951).

Besides the above organisations a number of departments in the State and Central Governments like Income Tax Department, Directorate General of Supplies and Disposals, Railways, Post and Telegraphs, Central Board of Revenues, Textile Commissioner's Office, Central Excise Commissioner's Office, Iron and Steel Controller's Office and so on, publish statistical reports on current problems and the information supplied by them is, in general, more authentic and reliable than that obtained from other sources on the same subject.

(ii) *Publications of Semi-Government Statistical Organisations:* Very useful information is provided by the publications of the semi-government statistical organisations, some of which are enumerated below:

— The Institute of Economic Growth, Delhi.
— Statistics department of the Reserve Bank of India (Bombay), which brings out an Annual Report of the Bank, Currency and Finance; Reserve Bank of India Bulletin (monthly) and various monthly and quarterly reports.

— The Institute of Foreign Trade, New Delhi.
— Economic department of Reserve Bank of India.
— Gokhale Institute of Politics and Economics, Pune.

Moreover, the statistical material published by the institutions like Municipal and District Boards, Corporations, Block and Panchayat Samitis on Vital Statistics (births and deaths), health, sanitation and other related subjects provides a fairly reliable and useful information.

(iii) *Publications of Research Institutions:* Individual research scholars, the different departments in the various universities of India and various research organisations and institutes like Indian Statistical Institute (I.S.I.), Kolkata and Delhi; Indian Council of Agricultural Research (I.C.A.R.), New Delhi; Indian Agricultural Statistics Research Institute (I.A.S.R.I.), New Delhi; National Council of Educational Research and Training (N.C.E.R.T.), New Delhi; National Council of Applied Economic Research (N.C.A.E.R.), New Delhi; The Institute of Applied Man Power Research, New Delhi; The Institute of Labour Research, Mumbai; Indian Standards Institute, New Delhi; and so on, publish the findings of their research programmes in the form of research papers, or monographs or journals which are a constant source of secondary data on the subjects concerned.

(iv) *Publications of Commercial and Financial Institutions*: A number of private commercial and trade institutions like Federation of Indian Chamber of Commerce and Industries (FICCI), Institute of Chartered Accountants of India, Trade Unions, Stock Exchanges, Bank Bodies, Cooperative Societies, etc., publish reports and statistical material on current economic, business and other phenomena.

(v) *Reports of Various Committees and Commissions.* The report of the survey and enquiry commissions and committees of the Central and State Governments to find their expert views on some important matters relating to economic and social phenomena like wages, dearness allowance, prices, national income, taxation, land, education, etc. are valuable source of secondary information. For instance, Simon-Kuznet Committee report on National Income in India, Wanchoo Commission Report on Taxation, Kothari Commission Report on Educational Reforms, Pay Commissions Reports, Land Reforms Committee Report, Gupta Commission Report on Maruti Affairs, Sarakaria Commission Report on Union-State Relations, etc., are authentic source of secondary data.

(vi) *Newspapers and Periodicals*: Statistical material on a number of important current socio-economic problems can be obtained from the numerical data collected and published by some reputed magazines, periodicals and newspapers like *Eastern Economist, Economic Times, The Financial Express, Indian Journal of Economics, Commerce, Capital, Transport, Statesman's Year Book, The Times of India Year Book,* and *Manorama Year Book,* etc.

(vii) *International Publications*: The publications of a number of foreign governments or international agencies provide invaluable statistical information on a variety of important economic and current topics. The publications of the United Nations Organisation (U.N.O.) like *U.N.O. Statistical Year Book, U.N. Statistical Abstract, Demographic Year Book,* etc. and its subsidiaries like World Health Organization (W.H.O.) On contagious diseases; annual reports of International Labour Organisation (I.L.O.); International Monetary Fund (I.M.F.); World Bank; Economic and Social Commission for Asia and Pacific, (E.S.C.A.P.); International Finance Corporation (I.F.C.); International Statistical Education Institute etc. are prestigious and important publications of authoritative secondary data.

Precautions in the Use of Secondary Data

It is highly desirable that a proper scrutiny of such data is made before they are used by the researcher. In fact, the use has to be extra-cautious while using secondary data. In this context, Prof. Bowley aptly states that "secondary data should not be accepted at their face value." The reason is that such data may be erroneous in many respects due to bias, inadequate size of the sample, substitution, errors of definition, arithmetical errors, etc. Even if there is non-error, such data may not be suitable and adequate for the purpose of the enquiry. Before using such data, the researcher should consider the following points:

(a) *Whether the data are adequate for the research:* Adequacy of the data is to be judged in the light of the requirements of the survey and the geographical area covered by the available data. For example, in the illustration given above, if our object is to study the wage rates of the workers in sugar industry in India and if the available data covers only the state of UP, it would not serve the purpose. The question of adequacy may also be considered in the light of the time period for which the data are available. For example, for studying trend of prices we may use data for the last 8-10 years from the source known to us data may be available for the last 2-3 years only which would not serve our object. It is found that the data are suitable for the purpose of research, they should be tested for adequacy.

(b) *Whether the data are suitable for the purpose of research in view:* The suitability of data can be judged in the light of the nature and scope of research. For example, if the object of enquiry is to study the wage levels including allowances of workers and the data relate to basic wages alone, such data should not be suitable for the immediate purpose. It may be difficult to find data which exactly fit the needs of the present project. Before using secondary data the researcher must ensure that the data are suitable for the purpose of the enquiry.

(c) *Whether the data are reliable:* Nodoubt, It is very difficult to assess whether the secondary data are reliable or not. The following tests if applied may be helpful to determine the reliability of the data:

— Was there a proper check on the accuracy of the field work?

— Were the enumerators capable and properly incompetent or poorly trained enumerators cannot be upon to produce useful result.

— Was the editing, tabulating and analysis carefully, and conscientiously done? Carelessness in either one or more of these functions can render or little value the findings of an otherwise valuable study.

— If the enumeration was based on a sample, was the sample representative?

— What degree of accuracy was desired by the compiler? How far was it achieved?

— Was the collecting agency unbiased or did it "have axe to grind"?

CHAPTER 9

Interpretation and Analysis of Data

On completion of data collection, the researcher concentrates his attention to their analysis. Analysis of data involves a number of closely interrelated operations that are performed to get answers to the research questions. Data collected are to be processed and analysed for a scientific conclusion and for ensuring that all relevant data are used for making contemplated comparisons and analysis. Processing of data implies editing, coding, classification and tabulation of collected data so that they are amenable to analysis. The term analysis refers to the computation of certain measures alongwith searching for pattern relationship among data groups.

Now, come to analysis of data and the processing of data. Processing of data refers to concentrating, recasting, and dealing with data so that they are as amenable to analysis as possible whereas analysis of data refers to seeing the data in the light of hypotheses or research question and the prevailing theories and drawing conclusion that are as amenable to theory formation, as far as possible. Thus, in the process of analysis, relationships or differences supporting or conflicting with original or new hypotheses should be subjected to statistical tests of significance to determine with what validity data can be said to indicate any conclusions." But there are many authors notably Selltiz, Jahoda and others, who do not like to make difference between the processing and analysis of data. According to this approach analysis of data in a general way involves a number of closely related operations which are performed with the purpose of summarizing the collected data and they are organised in such a manner that they are amenable to answer the research questions.

Processing Operations

This deals with concentrating, recasting and deal with data so that they are used for the analysis of the research problem under study. Processing operations are discussed below:—

1. Editing: The next step after collection of data in a statistical investigation is the scrutiny of these collected data. This is technically called editing of data. It is an essential step because in most of the collected data there is possibility of various types of mistakes and errors.

The process of scrutinizing the data to improve their quality for coding is known as editing. Thus editing is the process by which errors and omissions in the filled in questionnaires or in the observations noted inadequate, wrong or false entries are detected. It assures us that the data are accurate, consistent with other facts gathered, uniformly entered as complete as possible and have been well arranged to facilitate coding and tabulation. Editing aims at ensuring that the data have the following attributes: (1) Uniformity of data; (2) Accurate and reliable data; (3) Consistent with other facts; (4) Facilitate coding the tabulation; and, Complete data.

Editing is done at two points or stages. They are *field editing* and *central editing*. Field editing deals with the review of the reporting forms by the investigator for completing what the latter has written in abbreviated form at the time of recording the responses from the respondents. This sort of editing is necessary as the investigator's writing styles sometimes become difficult for others. This editing is done immediately after the interview has been conducted.

On the other hand, *Central editing* should be done when all questionnaires or schedules have been completed and returned to the office. Under this sort of editing all forms are thoroughly edited by a single editor in a small study and by a team of editors in case of a large research study. The editors may correct the obvious errors such as wrong entries made in the forms like weeks in place of months. Some missing replies can also be corrected either by going through the questionnaire or by contacting the respondent for clarification. All the wrong replies which seem to be obvious, must be dropped from the final results, especially in case of mail surveys.

Points to be Kept in Mild While Editi ng

1. The answers which are changed should be initialled by the editors themselves.
2. Data of editing and the initials of the editors should be placed on each completed form.
3. While crossing out and original entry in the questionnaire or schedule, they should just draw a single line on it which may remain legible.
4. Editors should be familiar with instructions given to the respondents and coders as well.
5. The entries on the form should be in some distinctive colour and a standardised form should be used by the editors.

2. *Coding:* Coding is regarded as the classification-process necessary for tabulation. It is the process of assigning numerals or other symbols to answers so that responses may be put into a limited number of categories or predetermined classes. These predetermined classes should be appropriate to the research problem under consideration. Through coding, the raw data are transformed into symbols that may be tabulated and counted. It is done by the 'coder.' 'Coder' is the official title for a person to whom the responsibility to give particular

codes to responds is assigned. According to Goode and Hatt coding is, "an operation by which data are organised into classes and a number of a symbol is given to each item, according to call class in which it falls." Coding is adopted where complex cross-tabulating occurs. It is done at any of the following states :—

1. The respondent himself may be asked to codify his own reaction. It is used in case of poll-type and multiple choice questions. For example, when the respondent is asked to indicate which of the classes (income groups) he belongs to, e.g. (a) below Rs. 800/- p.m. (b) Rs. 801 to Rs. 1000/- p.m. (c) Rs. 1001 to Rs. 1200/- p.m. (d) Rs. 1201/- and above. The respondent ticks off his position among the given alternatives.
2. The second stage at which the coding can be done when in the course of data collection, the interviewer or observer categorizes the subjects' responses. The interviewer may codify informants' reactions while recording them. It is used when an interviewer employs a rating scale to describe a respondent's response or behaviour.
3. The final stage of codification is in the office after the interviews are over based on the 'code book.' The data collected are deposited in the research office and official coders exercise their judgement to assign particular codes to particular responses. Whatever method of coding is adopted, one should see that coding errors are altogether quashed or reduced to the minimum level.

3. *Classification:* Classification is the process of arranging the data in related facts into classes according to homogenity and heterogenity. Data of one class differ from those of another class with reference to the basis of their classification. Prof. D.N. Elhance has defined, "The process of arranging data in groups or classes according to resemblances and

similarities is technically called classification. Thus, by classification we try to strike a note of homogeneity in the heterogeneous elements of the collected information." Thus in the process of data classification, units having a common feature are placed in one-class and in this fashion the whole data are divided into a number of classes.

Despite the fact that classification is an important preliminary in a statistical analysis no hard and fast rules can be laid down for it. The classification of data in each investigation has to be decided after taking into account the nature, scope and purpose of the enquiry or research problem. However, an ideal classification of data should be unambiguous, stable and flexible.

Statistical data are classified on the basis of the characteristics possessed by the different groups of units of a universe. Classification can be done depending upon the nature of the phenomenon involved and it can be one of the following two types :—

(a) *Classification according to attributes*: Data are classified on the basis of common characteristics which can either be descriptive or numerical. Unemployment, occupation, literacy, sex and honesty are examples of descriptive characteristics while age, weight, income, height are examples of numerical characteristics. Descriptive characteristics can be studied as qualitative phenomena which cannot be measured quantitatively. Only their presence or absence in an individual unit can be found out. For example, we cannot measure literacy in quantitative terms. Thus data obtained on the basis of certain attributes are known as statistics of attributes and their classification is called according to attributes.

Classification according to attributes can be of two types—simple classification and manifold classification. If the first method we consider only one attribute and divide the universe into two-classes—one class represents the items possessing the given attribute and other class represents the items which do not possess the given attribute. But in the Second method we consider two or more attributes simultaneously, and divide the data into a number of classes. For example, if the problem of blindness is studied sex-wise, there are two attributes under study, namely blindness and sex. A person can be either blind or not blind, further a person can be either a male or a female. Whenever data are classified qualitatively or according to attributes the researcher should see that the attributes are defined in such a manner that any doubt or ambiguity in the said attributes should be minimised.

(b) *Classification according to class-intervals*: Numerical characteristics refer to quantitative phenomena which can be measured through some statistical units. Data relating to height, weight, income, production and consumption etc. came under this category. Such data are also known as statistics of variables and are classified on the basis of class intervals. For example, persons whose incomes are between Rs. 301 and Rs. 500 can form one group, those whose incomes are between Rs. 501 and Rs. 700 can form another group and so on. In this way the entire data can be divided into a number of classes or groups which are technically known as class-intervals. These class-intervals have can upper as well as a lower limits. The difference between the upper limit and lower limit and lower limit or class interval is called class magnitude.

Classification according to class intervals involves three basic problems:

(i) Number of classes and their magnitude,

(ii) Choice of class limits

(iii) Counting the number in each class.

Number of Classes and Magnitude

There can be no specific answer with regard to the number

of classes and their magnitude. The skill and experience of the researcher will decide this. Ordinarily, a frequency distribution should not have more than 20 to 25 and not less than 6 to 8 classes, depending upon the total number of items of the series. Class intervals should be of equal magnitudes but in some cases unequal magnitudes may result in better classification. Hence the researcher's decision plays in important role in this connection. An ideal number of classes for any frequency distribution would be that which gives the maximum information in the clearest fashion.

The magnitude of class intervals depends on the range of the data and the number of classes. In the range (difference between the maximum and the minimum values) of the heights of a group of persons is 15," and it is desired to have 10 classes, the magnitude of each class interval would be 1.5." The magnitude of the class internals should be such that it does not exclude the important characteristics of the data. The multiples of 2.5 and 10 are generally preferred while determining the class intervals, H.A. Sturges has suggested the following formula for determining the size of the class interval which is adopted by some of the statisticians:

$$i = \frac{R}{1 + 3.3 \log N}$$

Where

i = Size of class intervals.
R = Range (i.e. difference between the maximum and minimum values of the class)
N = Number of items to be grouped.

Class Limits: The most important thing that should be kept in mind by the researcher while choosing the class limits is that these should be chosen in such a manner that the mid-point of a class interval and the actual average of items of that class interval should be as close to each other as possible. Consistent with this, the class limits should be located at multiples of 2, 5, 10, 20, 100 and such other figures class limits can be stated in any of the following forms :—

Exclusive type class intervals: Under this class interval, the items whose values are equal to the upper limit of a class are grouped in the next higher class. For exactly 20 would be put in 20-30 class interval and not in 10-20 class interval. In other words, we can say under exclusive type class intervals, the upper limit of a class interval is excluded and items with values less than the upper limit are put in the given class interval.

Inclusive type class intervals: In this type of class intervals the upper limit of a class interval is also included in the concerning class interval. Thus, an item whose value is 100 will be put in 100-190 class interval. The stated upper limit of the class intervals 100-190 is 190 but the real limit is 199.99 and as such 100-199 class interval really means 100 and under 200.

Frequency of each class: After deciding the number of classes, their magnitude and class limits, the next step comes counting the number of items falling in each class. This can be done either by tally sheets or by mechanical aids.

Under tally sheets method the class intervals are written on a sheet of paper called tally sheet and for each items a stroke is marked against the class interval in which it falls. Usually after every four strokes in a class, the fifth item is indicated by drawing flower. These groups of five are easily counted.

In case of large enquiries and surveys mechanical aids are used for counting the number of items in each class. Some of these machines are operated either by hand or with electricity. Needle sorting and punched cards are some of these aids. This method is less time consuming and expensive.

4. *Tabulation*: Tabulation is a part of the technical process

in the statistical analysis of the data. It is a technique of presenting data, either qualitative or quantitative in the column and rows. Professor Neis Wanger has defined tabulation as "a systematic organisation of data in columns and rows."

The technique of tabulation has the aim.

(i) To make the purpose of inquiry clear,
(ii) To facilitate the process of comparison,
(iii) To express the data in the least possible space,
(iv) To provide a basis for various statistical computations.
(v) to facilitate the detection of errors and omissions.

In the broadest sense tabulation is an orderly arrangement of data in columns and rows. It involves the systematic presentation of data to elucidate the problem under investigation. It is a process between the collection of data on the one hand, and its final analysis on the other. Thus tabulation is meant to properly arrange the answers relating to the question posed in any research problem and is very helpful in the analysis of the collected data as also in drawing inferences from them. Tabulation is the final process in the collection and compilation of data, and is a sort of stepping stone to the analysis and interpretation of data. In deciding about the type of tabulation the researcher has to keep in his mind the nature, scope and object of his research problem. Tabulation of data should be done in such a manner that it suits the nature and object of the research problem. The importance of proper tabulation is very great because if the tabulation is very great because if the tabulation of data is not satisfactory, its analysis will not only be difficult but the inferences drawn will be far from satisfaction of the researcher.

Types of Tabulation

Broadly speaking, tabulation of data can either Simple or Complex. Simple tabulation involves information about one or more groups of independent questions whereas complex tabulation shows the division of data in two or more categories and as such is meant to give information about one or more sets of inter-related questions.

One-way-Tables: Simple tabulation usually gives rise to single or one-way tables. These tables supply answers to questions about one characteristic of data only.

The above table tells us about the number of students in each class interval of marks obtained by them. We can know that 30 students obtained marks between 40 and 50 while 10 students obtained marks between 70 and 80. Thus this table gives us information only about one characteristic of data, that is, marks of students in statistics.

Two-way Tables: As against the one-way table there are double or two-way tables. The tables give information about two inter-related characteristics of a particular phenomenon. If the numbers of students given in the above table are further divided sex-wise the table would become a two-way table because it would give information about two characteristics, namely the marks obtained by students in statistics and the sex-wise distribution of students in various class intervals of marks. The table will be as follows :

The above table supplies information about questions relating to two inter-related phenomena. From the table we can find out that 30 students obtained marks between 40 and 50. Out of these students 10 were males and 20 were females. Similarly 30 students obtained marks between 60 and 70. Out of these 30 students 20 were males and 10 were females.

Three-way Tables: The tables are used to study three inter-related phenomena. A three-way table can answer questions relating to three-inter-related problems. In the above example if we further find out the number of students who were hostlers and the number who were day scholars a three-way table would be necessary. It will be as follows:

Thus the above table can supply us information about

(1) marks obtained by students (2) the distribution of these students sex-wise and (3) the distribution of the students on the basis of residence.

Higher order tables: The tables can also be manifold or of higher order. These tables supply information about a large number of interrelated questions. If in the above table additional information is given about civil conditions of the students, it would become a four-way table and similarly tables can be of still higher order-five-way, six-way, seven— and so on. All such tables are called manifold or higher order tables.

The above table gives information about a large number of inter-related questions regarding students, namely about the marks obtained sex-wise and on the basis of civil conditions and residence. These tables are very useful in presenting population census data.

Rules of tabulation: We have discussed the meaning, importance and types of tabulation. It is necessary to lay down certain rules or principles for the construction of tables. These rules may also be called the characteristics of a good table. They can be briefly stated as follows:

1. The table should be clear, precise, adequate and easy to understand. Its title should be clearly written.
2. Every table should be given a distinct number for the reference.
3. Each table should be complete in all respects and should serve a particular purpose.
4. The table should suit the size of the paper.
5. The units of measurement under each heading or sub-heading should be clearly indicated.
6. Explanatory footnotes concerning the table should be given beneath the table along with the reference symbols.

7. Sources of the data in the table should also be indicated just below the table.
8. There should be thick lines to separate the data under one class from the data under another class.
9. The columns of the table may be numbered to facilitate reference.
10. Those columns whose data are to be compared should be kept side by side.
11. The figures shown in the table should be approximated before tabulation.
12. Terms should be arranged either in alphabetical, chronological or geographical order or according to size, importance, emphasis or casual relationship to facilitate comparison.
13. If certain figures are to be emphasised they should be shown in distinctive type or in box or circle etc.
14. If some portion of collected data cannot be classified in any class a miscellaneous class should be created and the data shown in it.
15. Total of rows should normally be placed in the extreme right column and that of coloumns should be placed at the bottom.

It should be remembered that there cannot be any rigidity about these rules or principles of tabulation. Tables must suit the needs and requirements of the research. Bowley has correctly said that, "in collection and tabulation common sense is the chief requisite and experience the chief teacher."

Problems in Processing

There are two types of problems of processing the data which are faced by a researcher for analytical purposes. They are:

1. Problem of "Don't know" responses: While processing the data, the investigator often comes across some responses that are difficult to handle. One of the categories of such responses is `Don't know Response.' When the number of such responses is small, it hardly matters. But when it is relatively large in number, it becomes a matter of great concern in which case the question arises : Is the question which is related with the `Don't Know' response useless? The answer may be of two types viz. the respondent fails to know actually the answer of the question or the investigator may fail in obtaining the appropriate information. The second aspect of the question is very important and it reflects a failure of the question process.

The solution of the 'Don't know' or (DK) response is that the researcher should design better type of questions. Good report of the researcher with the respondents will help in minimising DK responses which have already occurred in the processing of data? One solution of the problem is to estimate the allocation of DK answers from other data in the questionnaire. The other way is to keep D.K. responses in a separate category in tabulation.

2. *Problem of using Percentages:* Percentages are used in data presentation. The simplify numbers, reducing all of them to a 0 to 100 range. It facilitates relative comparisons. A researcher should follow the following guidelines while using percentages in studying his research problem:

1. Two or more percentages should not be averaged. Each group size is given weightage and by ignoring the weightage given to each group the average will not give the correct result.
2. Use of too large percentages should be avoided because this sort of use will create confusion and defeat the very purpose for which percentages are used.
3. Base year of percentages should be kept in mind while studying the problem.
4. Descrease in percentages does not exceed 100.

5. While preparing two-dimension tables the percentages should be generally worked out will reference to casual-factor relationship.

Statistical Analysis of Data

In most of research studies a large volume of raw data are used and they are reduced so that the same may be read easily and can be used further analysis.

In fact, there are two major areas of statistics viz. descriptive statistics and inferential statistics. On the basis of these areas the analysis is also called descriptive and inferential analysis. Descriptive statistics deal with the development of certain indices from the new data. Whereas inferential statistics concern with the process of generalisation about some population on the basis of repeated observation. It is related with the estimation of population parameters and the testing of statistical hypotheses.

Statistics plays a very important role in research. There is hardly any research in these days where the statistical data and statistical methods are not used. The following are some important statistical measures which are used to summarise the research data:

1. Measures of central tendency or statistical averages;
2. Measures of dispersion;
3. Measures of asymmetry (skewness);
4. Measures of relationship, and
5. Miscellaneous measures.

Measures of central tendency deal with different types of averages such as mean median, mode, geometric and harmonic means. Geometric mean and harmonic means are sometimes used also.

In measures of dispersion, variance and its square root—the standard deviation are the most often used measures.

Other measures are mean deviation, range coefficient of standard deviation or the coefficient of variance.

Under the measures of skewness and kurtosis, we mostly use the first measure of skewness based on mean and mode or on mean and median. Other measures of skewness are based on quartiles methods of moments. Kurtosis is also used to measure the peakedness of the frequency distribution.

Measures of relationship deal with Karl Pearsons coefficient of correlation in case of statistics of attributes. Multiple correlation, coefficient, partial correlation coefficient, regression analysis etc. are other measures of relationship used by a researcher.

In case of other measures we study Index numbers, analysis of time series, coefficient of contingencies, etc. depending upon the nature of the research problem under study.

We will discuss below in brief some important measures often used in the context of research studies.

Measures of Central Tendency

Measures of central tendency of statistical averages deal with the point about which items have a tendency to cluster. Such a measure is considered as the most representative figure for the entire mass of data. They are also known as statistical average. They give a bird's eye view of the huge mass of statistical data which ordinarily are not easily intelligible. A series can be represented by an average only if the average is really typical. Average which are representative are called Typical Averages and those which are not representative and have only a theoretical value are called Descriptive averages.

Measures of central tendency of averages are of two types :

(a) Mathematical Averages

(i) Arithmetical Average
(ii) Geometric Mean
(iii) Harmonic Mean

(b) Averages of Position

(i) Median
(ii) Mode

(i) *Arithmetical Average*: Arithmetic Average or mean of a series is the figures obtained by dividing the total values of the various items by their number. If the marks of a group of eleven students are 64, 69, 63, 60, 68, 65, 62, 67, 70, 66 and 61, then to find the arithmetic average of the marks of these students we shall add these figures and divide the total so obtained, by the number of items which is 11. The total of the items in this example is 715 and if it is divided by 11 we get the figure of 65. This is the mean or arithmetic average of the series. We can work it out as under :

$$\text{Mean (or } \bar{x}) = \frac{\Sigma xi}{n} = \frac{x1 + x2 + \ldots .xn}{n}$$

Where $\bar{x}$ = Arithmetic mean or average
Σ = Symbol of summation
xi = value of the i th item x, i=1,2....n
n = total number of items.

In case of a frequency distribution, the mean can be calculated in this way :

$$\overline{X} = \frac{\Sigma fixi}{\Sigma fi} = \frac{F1x1 + f2x2 \ldots\ldots + fxn}{F1 + F2 + \ldots\ldots Fn = N}$$

Weighted mean for a realistic average can calculated as follows :

$$\overline{X}w = \frac{\Sigma wixi}{\Sigma wi}$$

Where $\overline{X}w$ = Weighted mean

wi = Weight of i th item X

xi = Value of the i th item x

The mean should be rigidly defined which leads to the value. It is based on all the observation of a series. Further algebric treatment is possible and it is easily calculated. It is least affected by fluctuations of sampling. But it has its demerits viz., it is usually affected by extreme items, it may not coincide with the actual value of an item in a series, and it may lead to wrong impression, particularly when the item values are not given with the average. However, the arithmetic mean is better than other averages, specially in economic and social studies where direct quantitative measurements are possible.

Median: Median is the value of the middle item of a series when it is arranged in ascending or descending order of magnitude. It is a point on a scale that half of the observations fall above it and half below it. If the values of the items arranged in the ascending order are : 60, 74, 80, 88, 90, 95, 100 then the value of the 4th item viz, 88 is the value of median. We can calculate this as follows :

$$\text{Median (M)} = \text{Value of } \frac{(n+1)}{(2)} \text{ th item}$$

Median is an ideal average as it is rigidly defined. It can be easily calculated and it is understood without any difficulty. It is not affected by the values of extreme items. It gives best results in a study of those phenomena which are incapable of direct quantitative measurement, for example intelligence. It suffers from some limitations viz. not representative when there are wide variations between the values of different items, algebric treatment is not possible, calculation of median in continuous series requires interpolation which is based on unrealistic assumption. It ignores the values of extreme items. It is not frequently used in sampling statistics.

Mode: Mode is the most common item of a series. The mode in a distribution is that item around which there is maximum concentration. In other words, mode is the size of the item which has the maximum frequency but at times such an item may not be mode on account of the effect of the frequencies of the neighbouring items. It is a positional average and is not affected by values of extreme items. When we talk of the 'average student, "the most common wage" the common man" or "the typical farm" and like, we are unconsciously referring to mode.

Mode cannot be calculated from a series of individual observations unless it is converted into either a discrete or continuous series. In a discrete series the value of the variable against which the frequency is the largest would be the model value. Similarly in case of a continuous frequency distribution the class-interval having the maximum frequency would be the model class. In a discrete series the value against which the frequency is the largest would be the modal value whereas in case of continuous series the mode is calculated on the basis of the following formula—

$$Z = L \quad \frac{f_1 - f_0}{f_1 - f_0 - f_2}$$

Where *Z* stands for the Mode, *L* is the lower limit of the modal class, f_0 stands for the frequencies of the preceding class, f_1 stands for the frequencies of the modal class, f_2 for the frequencies of the succeeding class and *i* stands for the class intervals of the modal class. Mode is also defined like this : Mode = 3 median—2 Mean. The mode like the median can be used as a central location for qualitative and quantitative data. Mode has the merits of simplicity commonly understood, most common item of a series, not affected by the values of extreme items, the determination does not require to know the values of all the items of a series. But is suffers from the following limitations—it is ill-defined, indeterminate and indefinite, not based on all the observations of a series, not capable of further mathematical treatment.

Geometric Mean: It is used to measure the average rate of change or growth for some quality. Geometric mean is the nth root of the product of n items of a series. It is used to find out the average percent increase in sales, population, production, economic and business series. Gêometric mean can be calculated on the basis of the following formula if the number of items is very few :—

$$g = n\sqrt{m^1 \times m^2 \ldots\ldots\ldots\ldots\ldots \times mn}$$

where g stands for the geometric mean.

n for the number of items and m for the values of variables.

If the number of items is large and their size is big, the calculation is done with the help of logs. In terms of logs—

$$\text{Log } g = \frac{\log m^1 + \log m^2 \ldots\ldots\ldots\ldots + \log mn}{n}$$

$$g = \text{Antilog } \frac{(\log m^1 + \log m^2 \ldots\ldots\ldots\ldots + \log mn)}{n}$$

or

$$\text{Anti} + \log\left(\frac{\Sigma \log m}{n}\right)$$

It is rigidly defined based on all the observations of a series, capable of further algebric treatment, and is not affected by the fluctuations of sampling. It has the demerits of being neither easy to calculate nor simple to understand. Moreover, it cannot be calculated when the value of a series is zero, may give a value which does not exist in the series; giving more weight to smaller items may prove to be a drawback of the geometric mean.

Harmonic Mean: Harmonic mean of a series is the reciprocal of the arithmetic average of the reciprocals of the values of its various items. It is calculated on the basis of the following formula :

$$h = \text{Reciprocal} \frac{\frac{1}{m_1} + \frac{1}{m_2} \text{........} + \frac{1}{mn}}{n}$$

Where h stand for the harnomic mean, m_1, m_2 etc. for the values of the variables and n for the number of items. It is used in cases where time and rate are involved. It gives largest weight to the smallest item and smallest weight to the largest item. As such this mean is used in studying the time and motion where time is variable and distance is constant.

Harmonic mean has the merits of the test of rigid definition, based on all the observations of series, not affected by fluctuations of sampling; it measures relative changes and is extremely useful in averaging certain types of ratios and rates.

It suffers from the demerits of being not readily understood nor can it be calculated with ease, gives very high weightage to small items and for analysis of economic data it is not very useful, it gives a value which does not exist in a series.

We have discussed various types of statistical averages. They have their merits and demerits. A researcher, has to make a choice for some statistical averages taking into account the nature, type and objectives of the research study. One particular type of average can not be taken as appropriate for all types of studies.

Measures of Dispersion: Average has its own limitations and even an ideal average can represent a series only "as best as a single figure can." Professor DN Elhance has rightly pointed out that "No doubt averages have a very great utility in statistical analysis but they fail to reveal the entire story of a phenomenon. There may be a dozen series whose averages may be identical but which may differ from each other in a hundred ways." Dispersion measures the degree to which the measurements vary from central value. In other words, it is the scatter or variability in a set of data. Prof. Bowley defines dispersion as "the measure of the variation of the items." Dispersion determines the reliability of an average, serves as basis for the control of variability, compares two or more series with regard to their variability, facilitates the use of other statistical measures. Thus dispersion not only gives a general impression about the variability of a series but also a precise measure of this variation.

Dispersion is studied through the following :—

1. Range
2. Inter-Quartile-Range
3. Semi-Inter-Quartile-Range or Quartile Range
4. Average Deviation or Mean Deviation
5. Standard Deviation.

Range: Range is the simplest possible measure of dispersion and is defined as the difference between the values of the extreme items of a series. Thus if in a series relating to the weight measurements of a group of students the lightest student has a weight of 80 pounds and the heaviest of 200 pounds, the value of range would be 120 pounds. Thus :

Range = highest observed value = lowest observed value of a series.

If range is divided by the sum of the extreme items the resulting figure is called "The ratio of the range" or "The coefficient of the scatter." The range has the only merit that it can be easily calculated and readily understood. It suffers from the demerits like that it is affected very greatly by fluctuations of sampling. Its value is never stable and it varies from one sample to another. It is not based on all the observations of series. Thus range is mostly used as a rough measure of variability and is not considered as an appropriate measure in series related with research studies.

Inter-Quartile Range: If the difference in the values of two quartiles is calculated it would give us what is known as Inter-Quartile Range, Quartile means Quarter of the data set. It (IQR) indicates the difference between the values of the first and the third quartiles and this difference indicates the range of the middle half of the data set. This measure of dispersion is not affected by the values of the extreme items. In fact 50 percent of the values of a variable are between the two quartiles and as such the IQR gives a fair measure of variability. It has its own limitations viz. it is affected by fluctuations of sampling and is not based on all the observations of sampling and is not based on all the observations of a series. It is measure of location and its value is not very stable. It ignores the composition of a series.

Semi-Inter-Quartile Range: It is the mid-point of the inter-quartile range. SIQR is one half of the difference between the third quartile and first quartile. It is calculated like this—

Semi-Inter-Quartile range

or

$$\text{Quartile deviation} = \frac{Q_3 - Q_1}{2}$$

Where Q_3 and Q_1 stand for the upper and lower quartiles respectively.

Quartile deviation is an absolute measure of dispersion. If it is divided by the average value of the two quartiles, a relative measure of dispersion is obtained. It is known as coefficient of Quartile Deviation.

Symbolically

$$\text{Coefficient of a quartile deviation } \frac{\frac{Q_3 - Q_1}{2}}{\frac{Q_2 + Q_3}{2}} = \frac{Q_3 - Q_1}{Q_3 + Q_1}$$

Quartile deviation has the merits of simple calculation and easily understand ability. But this measure of dispersion is neither based on all the observations of data nor is it capable of further algebric treatment. It is also affected to a considerable extent by the fluctuations of sampling. In series having considerable variation, the measure is not suitable.

Average/Mean Deviation: The above measures of dispersion suffer from one serious limitation, i.e. they are calculated by taking into account only two value of a series. They ignore other values of a series. They are not based on all the observations of a series. Thus for taking into account all the observations of a series and calculating in relating to a central value, average or mean deviation is used. Mean deviation of a series is the arithmetic average of the deviations of various items from a measure of central tendency like mean, median or mode. Deviations are taken from any of the three averages but in practice it is taken from mean and median only because in case of mode the value is indeterminate and its conclusions are not correct. Mean deviation is also called as the first moment of dispersion. It is calculated on the basis of the following formula :

$$\text{(i) } \delta = \frac{\Sigma d}{n}$$

Where δ stands for the mean deviation, d for the deviations from the mean, and n for the number of items.

$$\text{(ii) } \delta m = \frac{\Sigma dm}{n}$$

Where δm stands for the mean deviation from median, *dm* for the deviations from the median, and *a* for the number of items.

$$\text{(iii) } \delta z = \frac{\Sigma dz}{n}$$

Where δz stands for the mean deviation from mode, *dz* for deviations from the mode, and *n* for the number of items.

The calculation of mean deviation with the above method will give us absolute measure of dispersion. In order to have a relative measure, it is divided by the average from which it has been calculated. It is known as the Mean coefficient of dispersion.

Thus, mean coefficient of dispersion from mean, median and mode would be like this :

$$\frac{\delta}{a}, \frac{\delta m}{M} \text{ and } \frac{\delta z}{Z}$$

Mean deviation has the merits of being precise and definite, easy to calculate, based on all the observations of a series, not affected by the values of the extreme items, ignoring the algebric signs of the deviations. But it is not a very accurate measure of dispersion particularly when it is calculated from the mode. Thus, this measure of dispersion is not in common use and generally dispersion is studied through standard deviation. Economists and businessmen have used favourably it due to its simplicity in calculation.

Standard Deviation: The technique of the calculation of mean deviation is mathematically illogical as in its calculation the algebric signs (+ or –) are ignored. Standard deviation is the most widely used measure of dispersion of a series and it is defined as the square root of the arithmetic average of the squares of the deviations measured from the mean. For the calculation of standard deviation first of all the arithmetic average is calculated and the deviations of various items from the arithmetic average are squared later on. Thus squared deviations are totalled and the sum is divided by the number of items. The square root of resulting figure is the standard deviation of the series. It is calculated as under :

$$\sigma = \sqrt{\frac{\Sigma d^2}{n}}$$

Where σ stands for the standard deviation, Σd^2 for the sum of the squares of the deviations measured from the arithmetic average and n for the number of items.

Calculation of standard deviation in a discrete series is done by squaring of the deviations from the arithmetic average multiplies by the respective frequencies of these items. The total of these products is divided by the total of the frequencies and square root of this figure is the standard deviation of the series. It is worked out as under—

$$\sigma = \sqrt{\frac{\Sigma fd^2}{n}}$$ f is the frequency of the item.

In case of continuous series standard deviation is calculated on the basis of the formula given below :

$$\sigma = \sqrt{\frac{\Sigma f\, x^2}{n} - \frac{(\Sigma fdx)^2}{n}} \times i$$

Where dx stands for the deviations in class-intervals and other signs stand for what they stood in the previous formulate.

Standard deviation is rigidly defined and its value is always definite. It is based on all the observations of a series. Its algebric treatment is possible and is less affected by the fluctuations of sampling. However, it has some limitations like being not easy to calculate nor is it easily understood, gives more weight to extreme items and less to those which are near the mean. In spite of these merits and demerits, it is the best measure of dispersion and should be used wherever possible. But it has not found favour with economists and businessman because it gives greater weight to extreme items and economists and businessmen are more interested in the results of the modal class.

Measures of Skewness

The measures of central tendency and dispersion do not reveal whether the dispersal of values on either side of an average is symmetrical or not. When the distribution of items in a series happens to be perfectly symmetrical, we can have the following type of curve for the distribution which is technically known as a normal curve and the relating distribution as normal distribution.

The above curve is a normal curve showing no skewness in which case we have X=M=Z. It gives a symmetrical distribution. A normal curve has many mathematical properties. If the curve is distorted whether on the right side or on the left side, we have asymmetrical distribution which indicates that there is skewness. If the curve is distorted on the right side, the skewness will be positive while if the distortions are towards left, the skewness will be negative.

In case of positive skewness we have Z M X whereas in case of negative skewness the position would change and it would be like this : $\overline{X}$ M Z.

Thus skewness is a measure of asymmetry and shows the manner in which the items are clustered around the average. In a symmetrical distribution, the items of a series show a perfect balance on either side of mode, but in a skew distribution the balance is thrown to one side. Measures of skewness give an idea about the extent of asymmetry in a series. They are also called measures of asymmetry.

First measures of skewness: These measures are based on the assumption that in a skew distribution the values of mean, median and mode do not coincide. The difference between any two of these values indicates the extent of skewness. Thus first measures of skewness are :

(i) Mean-Mode or (a–z)
(ii) Mean-Median or (a–m)
(iii) Median-Mode (M–z)

The above measures of skewness are absolute measures. For the purpose of comparison it is necessary to have relative measures of skewness are calculated by dividing the absolute measures by any measures of dispersion. The relative measures of skewness are known as co-efficient of skewness.

Thus Coefficient of skewness or

$$j = \frac{a - z}{\delta Z} \text{ or } j = \frac{a - z}{\delta}$$

If mode is ill-defined median can be used in place of mode and then :

$$j = \frac{a - M}{\delta m} \text{ or } j = \frac{a - M}{\delta}$$

Skewness can also be studied by studying the difference of median and mode. Thus,

$$j = \frac{M - z}{\delta z} \text{ or } j = \frac{M - Z}{\delta m}$$

Karl Pearson has given a formula in which the denominator is not the mean deviation but standard deviation.

Thus $j = \frac{a - z}{\delta}$

As we have seen that in a moderately asymmetrical distribution :

Mean-Mode=3 (Mean-Median)

$$\text{Thus } j = \frac{3(a-M)}{\sigma}$$

Second Measure of Skewness: It is based on the quartiles. It has been said that in a skewed distribution ($M-Q_1$) and (Q_3-M) would not be equal. A measure of skewness is thus derived by finding out the difference between these two values.

Thus

$$\begin{aligned}\text{Second measure of skewness} &= (Q_3-M)-(M-Q_1)\\ &= Q_3-2M+Q_1\\ &= Q_3+Q_1-2M\end{aligned}$$

Above is an absolute measure of skewness. The relative measure can be derived by dividing this absolute measure by the sum of (Q_3-M) and ($M-Q_1$). Thus the coefficient of skewness would be as follows :

$$i = \frac{(Q_3-M)-(M-Q_1)}{(Q_3-M)+(M-Q_1)}$$

$$= \frac{Q_3+Q_1-2M}{Q_3-Q_1}$$

This coefficient gives us a pure number. Its theoretical limits are ± 1. In case of a symmetrical distribution its value would be zero (0). The second measure of skewness and its coefficient do not always give dependable results. The reason for this is that quartiles are not based on all the observations of a series. Thus this measure of skewness should be used with caution by the researcher and for purposes of comparison Karl Pearson's coefficient of skewness should be used.

The measures of skewness have their significance. The researcher can study the formation of series and can have the idea about the shape of the curve, whether it is a normal curve or not.

Kurtosis: The measures of skewness tell us whether a particular distribution differs from a normal or symmetrical distribution and if so, to what extent. Another measure used to know how far a particular frequency distribution conforms to the normal curve is called Kurtosis. This measure indicates whether a distribution is more flat-topped or more peaked than the normal distribution.

Curve No. 1 is a normal curve. It is also called Meso Kurtic. Curve No. 2 is mere peaked than the normal curve. Such curves are called Lepto Kurtic. Curve No. 3 is more flat-topped than the normal curve and it is called platy kurtic.

Kurtosis is measured by coefficient β_2 or its derivation y_2.

$$Y_2 = \beta_2 - 3$$

The standard value of β_2 is taken as 3 and the curves with values or β_2 less than 3 are called platy kurtic and curves with values of β_2 more than 3 are called leptokurtic. In a normal or Mesokurtic curve the value of β_2 is equal to 3. As such for a normal curve the value of y_2=0 and in curves which are more flat-topped or more peaked than the normal curve the value of y_2 in a frequency distribution, the greater is its departure from normality.

Measures of Relationship

So far we have discussed those statistical measures that are used in the context univariate population or the population consisting of measurement of only one variable. But when there are two variables these measures are useless and we have a bivariate population and if the data happen to be one more than two variables, the population is known as multivariate population. These measures of relationship are studied under correlation, regression, association of attributes.

Correlation: Correlation measures the degree of relationship between the variables under the consideration. Ya Lun Chou has defined correlation as "the degree of relationship between variables. "Prof. Elhance opines that," the term correlation or co-variation indicates the relationship between two such variables in which with changes in the values of one variable the values of the other variable also change." The change leads to change in the relationship of two variables. This relationship may change either on account of their mutual interdependence or cause-effect relationship or effects of a third factor. The correlation helps us in :

(a) determining whether a relation exists
(b) Testing whether it is significant, and
(c) Establishing the cause effect relation, if any.

In natural and physical sciences the study of correlation is not very difficult, as on the basis of experiments, mathematical relationship can be established between the values of two or more variables. But in case of economics and other social sciences the study of correlation cannot be so accurate and precise because they are inexact sciences and human factor plays a very important role. Here the data are affected by multiplicity of causes and it becomes difficult to ascertain which particular cause is responsible for changes in the value of a variable.

When the values of two variables move in the same direction so that an increase in the value of one variable is associated with an increase in the value of the other variable also, and a decrease in the value of one variable is associated with the decrease in the value of the other variable also, the correlation is called positive correlation. The relationship between the price of a commodity and its quantity supplied is an example of this type of correlation. If the values of two variable move in different directions so that with an increase in the value of one variable the value of the other variable decreases and with a decrease in the value of one variable the value of the other variable increases, the correlation is called negative correlation. The relationship between the price of a commodity and its quantity demanded is an example of negative correlation because when the price decreases the quantity demanded increases and versa.

correlation in two more series can be studied by any one of the following methods :

(a) scatter diagram
(b) correlation graphs
(c) coefficient of correlation
(d) correlation table.

Coefficient of correlation is calculated to study the extent or degree of correlation between two variables. Karl Pearson, the great biologist and statistician has given a formula for the calculation of coefficient of correlation. According to it the coefficient of correlation of two variables is obtained by dividing the sum of the products of the correspondence deviation of the various items of two series from their respective means by the product of their standard deviations and the number of pairs of observations. Karl Pearson's formula of coefficient of correlation is :

$$r = \frac{\Sigma xy}{n\sigma^1\sigma^2}$$

Where *xy* stands for product of deviation of *x* and *y* series, *n* stands for the number of pairs of observations of *x* and y, σ^1 stands for standard deviation of *x* and σ^2 stands of standard deviation of *y*.

In case of series of individual observations the following formula can be used—

$$r = \sqrt{\frac{\Sigma xy}{\Sigma x^2 . \Sigma y^2}}$$

Where

R	=	Coefficient of correlation
Σxy	=	Total of product of deviations of x and y taken from their averages
Σx^2	=	square of x series
Σy^2	=	Square of deviation of y series.

In case of short cut method in such series the formula which is used is :

$$r = \frac{\Sigma xy - \frac{\Sigma x . \Sigma y}{n}}{\sqrt{(\Sigma x^2 - \frac{(\Sigma x)^2}{n} \quad (\Sigma y^2 - \frac{(\Sigma y)^2}{n}}}$$

The Karl Pearson's coefficient of correlation is based on two assumptions :—

1. A large number of independent contributory causes are operating in each of the two series correlated, so as to produce normal or probability distribution. We know that such causes always operate in chance phenomena like tossing of coin or throw of a dice.
2. The forces so operating are not independent of each other but are related in a casual fashion.
3. There is linear relationship between the two variables.

Coefficient of correlation by rank differences is calculated on the basis of the following formula—

$$r = 1 - \frac{6(\Sigma d^2)}{n(n^2 - 1)} \quad \text{or} \quad 1 - \frac{6(\Sigma d^2)}{n^3 - n}$$

Where r stands for the co-efficient of correlation; Σd^2 for the total of the squares of the difference of corresponding ranks, and n for the number of pairs of observations.

Coefficient of concurrent deviation can also be calculated on the basis of the following formula—

$$r = \pm\sqrt{\left(\pm\frac{2c - n}{n}\right)}$$

Where r stands for the coefficient of concurrent deviations, c for the number of pairs of concurrent deviations and n for the number of pairs of deviations. The value of this coefficient of correlation also varies between –1 and + 1.

Regression: Regression is the determination of a statistical relationship between two or more variables. According to Ya Lun Chou regression means "the nature of the relationship between variables." It measures the average relationship between two or more variables in original terms. The regression analysis helps us in estimating or predicting the unknown value of one variable. The variable which is used for predicting the variable of interect is called independent variable or explanatory variable. The variable for which one tries to predict is called dependent variable or explained variable. The procedure to accomplish in finding the value of dependent variable from the independent variable is called 'regression line' or 'regression equation.' The variation in the dependent variable alongwith the independent variable may either be positive or negative and it is called regression coefficient. The equation for the calculation of lines is : $y = a + bx$.

Regression equation of x on y would be used to describe the variation in the values of x for given changes in the values of y, and similarly the regression equation of y on x

would be used to describe the variation in the values of y for given changes in the values of x. If the variations are studied from the respective means of the two series the regression equations would be calculated as follows :—

Regression equation of x only

$$x = a + by$$

This equation can also be written in terms of the coefficient of correlation, standard deviations and the means of two series.

$$X - \overline{X} = r\frac{\sigma^x}{\sigma^y}(y - \overline{y})$$

Where $\overline{X}$ and $\overline{Y}$ stand for the mean values of x and y series and x and y for their standard deviations and r for the coefficient of correlation.

Regression equation of y on x

$y = a + bx$ or

$$y - \overline{y} = r\frac{\sigma y}{\sigma y}(y - \overline{y})$$

The symbols stand for the same things as in the previous case.

Regression equations deal with mean values of the two series and indicate the variation in one series from its mean as compared to a variation from the mean of the other series regression coefficient gives the value by which one variable changes for a unit change in the other variable. As we have studied that just as there are two regression equations similarly there are two regression coefficient. The regression coefficient of x and y would indicate the value by which x variable would change as compared to a unit change in the value of y variable. Similarly the regression coefficient of y on x

would indicate the value by which the y variable would change as compared to a unit change in x variable. The regression coefficients are calculated as follows :—

Regression Coefficient on x of y =

$$r\frac{\sigma x}{\sigma y}$$

Regression Coefficient of y of x =

$$r\frac{\sigma y}{\sigma x}$$

An important point that should be kept in mind by the researcher about the regression coefficients is that the values of both the regression coefficients individually can not exceed unity, though the value of one of the regression coefficient can be more than unity. If the values of both the regression coefficients are more than 1, the value of the coefficient of correlation which is equal to the square root of the product of the regression coefficients, would also be more than 1.

Multiple Correlation and Regression: Where there are two or more than two independent variables, the analysis of such relationship is known as multiple correlation and the equation describing such relationship is called the multiple regression equation. In regression analysis we study the independent variable effect on a dependent variable. This is possible only in areas like height of fathers and sons, rainfall and production etc. But it cannot be used when there is a dependent variable with a number of independent variables. For example, production in the farm sector is the result of good rainfall, quality of seed, fertilisers etc. Multiple regression analysis helps us to measure the collective effect of all these independent variables on the dependent variables. It studies the average relationship between these independent variables and the dependent variables.

Multiple regression equation is given below :

$$Y = a + b_1 x_1 + b_2 x_2$$

Where x_1 and x_2 are two independent variables and y being the dependent variable and the constant a, b^1 and b_2 can be solved by solving the following three normal equations:—

$$\Sigma yi = na + b_1 \Sigma x_1 i + b_2 \Sigma 2i$$

$$\Sigma x_1 iyi = a\Sigma x_1 i + b_1 \Sigma x^2_1\ i + b_2 \Sigma x_i ix2i$$

$$\Sigma x2iyi = a\Sigma 2i + b_1 \Sigma x1ix2i + b_2 \Sigma x^2_1$$

Association of Attributes

Measures of central tendency, measures of dispersion and skewness, correlation and regression are some of the important statistical methods by which the data can be analysed in quantitative terms and they are known as statistics of variables. Contrary to it, data might be such that it is not possible for the researcher to measure their magnitude. In such cases the researcher can only study the presence of absence of a particular quality in a group of individuals. For example data related with blindness, insanity, deaf-mutism, sickness, honestly, extravagance etc. are the attributes where the researcher can not measure the magnitude of the data. What can do is to count the number of persons who are honest. Thus such data in which the quantitative measurement of the magnitude is not possible and in which only the presence or absence of an attribute can be studied are called statistics of attributes. In such a situation our interest may be limited to know whether the attributes are associated with each other or not.

The association may be positive or negative. If the class frequency of AB written as (AB), is greater than the expectation of AB being together if they are independent, then we say the two attributes are positively associated and if the class frequency of AB is less than this expectation, the two attributes are negatively associated. In case the class frequency of AB is equal to expectation, the two attributes are considered as independent. It can be concluded like this:

If $(AB) > \frac{(A)}{N}.\frac{(B)}{N} \times N$, then AB are positively associated.

If $(AB) < \frac{(A)}{N}.\frac{(B)}{N} \times N$, then AB are negatively associated.

If $(AB) = \frac{(A)}{N}.\frac{(B)}{N} \times N$, then AB are independent or they have no association.

Where (AB) stands for frequency of class (AB), $\frac{(A)}{N}.\frac{(B)}{N} \times N$ are expectation of AB, if A and B are independent, and N being the number of items.

In order to find out the degree or intensity of association between two or more sets of attributes, we can calculate it with the help of the coefficient of association. Professor Yule has developed and given the formula for the coefficient of association. It is like this:

$$QAB = \frac{(AB)\,(ab) - (Ab)\,(a\beta)}{(AB)\,(ab) + (Ab)\,(aB)}$$

Where

QAB stands for Yule's coefficient of association between attributes of A and B.

(AB) stands for frequency of class AB in which A and B are present.

(AB) stands for frequency of class Ab in which A is present but B is absent.

(aB) stands for frequency of class aB in which A is absent

but B is present.

(ab) stands for frequency of class ab in which both A and B are absent.

The value of this coefficient will be some where between + 1 and –1.

The arrangement of frequencies falling within the different classes called 'contingency table.' The coefficient of contingency is calculated with the help of the following formula :—

$$C = \sqrt{\frac{X_2}{N + X^2}}$$

$$X^2 = \frac{\Sigma(O - E)^2}{E}$$

C is coefficient of contingency

Where—

O = Observed frequency
E = Expected frequency
N = Total value.

In order to judge the significance of association between two attributes, we can use chi-square test by using the value of chi-square (X^2) and using chi-square distribution.

Association can also be studied in contingency table through Yule's coefficient of association and for this purpose we have to reduce the contingency table into 2 × 2 table by combining some classes. But in practice this method is not considered very correct and at times it is inconvenient also. Karl Person has suggested a measure for studying association in contingency table which is known as coefficient of mean square contingency. This is calculated like this :

$$C = \sqrt{\frac{X^2}{X^2 + N}}$$

Where C is coefficient of contingency, x^2 is chi-square value which is $= \frac{\Sigma(O-E)^2}{E}$ and N = Number of items.

Other Measures

The other statistical measures which are used by the researcher are discussed below:—

Index Numbers: An Index Number is statistical measure designed to show changes in a variable or a group of related variables over time or with respect to other characteristics. Index numbers are used to study the changes in the effects of such factors which cannot be measured directly. Professor Bowley opines that, "Index Numbers are used to measure the changes in some quantity which we cannot observe directly." For example, changes in business activity in India are not capable of direct measurement but it is possible to study relative changes in business activity by studying the variations in the values of some such factors which affect business activity and which are capable of direct measurement.

Changes in various economic and social phenomena can be measured through the technique of index numbers. Different index numbers serve different purposes. We can study the general price level, cost of living, industrial activity etc. Their direct quantitative measurement is not possible. We can study their relative changes by studying the variations in certain other factors which are connected with these problems.

Index Numbers are useful for various reasons. They are:

1. Index Numbers help in framing right policy. For example while fixing the dearness allowance for

employees has to depend on the cost of living index.

2. Index numbers reveal trends and tendencies of social, economics phenomena which are studied. For example, if we want to study the trends and tendencies of India's foreign trade we can study the index numbers related to India's foreign trade.
3. They are also useful to adjust the original data. For example, the nominal wages can be converted into real wages.

While constructing price indices we are faced with various problems. They are :—

1. Selection of items to be included in the index numbers.
2. Selection of the base year,
3. Selection of the average,
4. Selection of suitable weights,
5. Selection of the sources from which information is to be collected,
6. Collection of the price of commodity from all markets in the country.

According to base method the index numbers are classified into—

1. Fixed base Method
2. Chain base Method

In the first case base period remains the same on the basis of which index is calculated for all the times whereas in the latter the base period is the preceding year. The chain base method provides us a better picture than what it obtained by the fixed base method.

Formula for calculating Index by chain base =

$$\frac{\text{Current year price}}{\text{Previous year price}} \times 100$$

Formula for calculating Index by fixed base =

$$\frac{\text{Current year Price}}{\text{Base year price}} \times 10^{\cap}$$

Regarding Weighting of index numbers it is essential that weight should be rational, that rational weights are usually money values and lastly, that weights should be fluctuating. Various formulate for calculating weighted index number have been developed. Some of them are :—

Laspeyers Method: In this method weights are determined quantities in the base period. This method is widely used because it keeps the quantities consumed in the base period as constant in the current period also and finds the change in aggregate value. But the demerit of this method is that it assumes quantities of the current year as given.

$$\text{The formula is POL} = \frac{\Sigma \text{PLqI}}{\Sigma \text{POqO}} \times 100$$

POL = Price Index, PO = Price of base year, PL = price of current year, qo = quantity of the base year and q^1 = quantity of the current year.

Paasche Method: In this method, the price of change is determined by quantities in the current year. The formula for constructing index is

$$\text{POL} = \frac{\Sigma \text{PLQI}}{\Sigma \text{POQL}} \times 100$$

Fisher Ideal Index: It is the geometric mean of the Laspeyer's and Pasche indices. The formula is

$$\text{POL} = \sqrt{\text{L} \times \text{P}}$$

Analysis of Variance: The analysis of variance indicates variation in nature of data. It consists of classifying and cross-classifying statistical results and testing the means of a specified classification whether differs significantly or not. Thus, it is used to test for the significance of the difference between two sample variance. The square of the standard deviation, or the arithmetic average of the squares of deviation taken from the mean is called variance. The analysis of variance was developed very elaborately theoretically by R.N. Fisher and now it is used in natural and social science.

$$\text{Variance or } V = \sigma^2$$

$$= \frac{\Sigma(-\overline{x})^2}{n-1}$$

Where x stands for the values of individual items, x for mean of the series and n for the total number of items. The degrees of freedom in small samples are equal to n–1. In other words, in small samples, standard deviation or

$$\sigma = \sqrt{\frac{\Sigma(X-\overline{X})}{n-1}}$$

$$\text{and variance of} = \frac{\Sigma(X-\overline{X})}{n-1}$$

The analysis of variance in simplified from called ANOVA and was developed by R.A. Fisher. The ANOVa is of two type, viz. one-way classification and two-way classification. The one-way classification deals with the variation between the samples while the ıatter reveals the variation between the sample samples as well as among the samples. The calculated value is compared to the table value. If it is more than the table value, it signifies the variation in samples is significant or otherwise not significant. Thus there are two types of variations in data one between the various samples and the other within the various samples. Now if the variations within the samples and between the samples are not significantly different from each other, the samples belong to the same universe, because variation between the samples is just like variations within the sample. In such a case if the researcher had taken only one sample of 20 items it would not have made any difference so far as variation of items is concerned. If, however, the variation within the samples is much greater than the variation within the samples it means that the samples it means that the samples come from different types of universes otherwise there would not have been a significant difference in the variations between the samples and within the samples. Thus the analysis of variance studies the relationship of the variation between the samples and the variation within samples.

Variation ratio can be calculated on the basis of the following formula—

$$F = \frac{\text{Variance between samples } (V_2)}{\text{Variance within samples } (V_1)}$$

The variance ratio or F has a very important property that its value remains unchanged if all the figures are either multiplied or divided by a common factor or if a common factor is added to or subtracted from each figure.

Probability: The analysis of artificial data which are obtained by methods which are more or less in our control gives us certain generalisations which are of very great use in statistics. These generalisations are studied under the theory of probability.

Mathematically the measure of probability can be defined in this way :—

"If an even can happen in m ways and fail to happen in *n* ways, and each of these ways is equally likely, the probability or the chance of its happening or $p = \frac{m}{(m+n)}$ and that of its failing to happen or $q = \dfrac{m}{(m+n)}$.

Thus the probability of happening of an event is equal to the number of ways favorable to the event divided by the total number of ways in which the event can happen and not happen.

There are three different approaches to probability theory. They are :

1. Classical or priori approach
2. Subjective approach
3. Relative frequency approach

Classical approach to probability is the oldest and simplest one. It is closely related with the problem of games of chance such as throwing of coins, dice or deck or cards etc. the formula is

$$p = \frac{a}{n}$$

Where p stands for probability, a stand for number of favourable cases and n = total number of equally likely cases.

Subjective approach to the theory of probability represents the degree of belief of an individual in a particular event of proposition. The degree of belief must conform to the generally accepted laws of probability. Subjective approach to the theory or probability is defined as the probability assigned to an event by an individual, based on whatever evidence is available.

Relative Frequency Approach is based on the observed relative frequency of an event in a very large number of trials or the proposition of times that an event occurs in the long run when conditions are stable. It is used to find out the occurrence of past probabilities. This approach is entirely based on empirical evidence that it why it is called objective.

Thus probability is very useful for decision making. It helps us in construction of econometric models, managerial decisions on planning and control with occurrence of all kinds. In It has become an indispensable technique for all types of formal studies that involve uncertainty.

Time Series Analysis: In the field of economic and business researches, we may collect data relating to some time period concerning a given phenomenon. Such data are studied in 'Time series.' Such studies which relate to the analysis of time series. A time series are usually the result of the effect of one or more of the following factors:

(a) Short term fluctuations consisting of seasonal variations and cyclical variations/fluctuations.
(b) Irregular or random fluctuations.
(c) Secular Trend.

The analysis of time series is based on two models :

(a) Additive Model
(b) Multiplicative Model

Additive model deals with the total of various components resulting in the given values, of the overall time series and can be found out as follows :

$$Q = T+C+S+I$$

In case of the multiplicative model we assume that the various components interact in a multiplicative manner to produce the given values of overall time series and they can be stated as under :

$$Y = TXCXSXI$$

Where *Y* is observed values of time series, *T* is Trend, C is cyclical fluctuations, S is Seasonal fluctuations and I is irregular fluctuations.

There are various methods of isolating trend for the given series. They are free hand method, semi-average method, Method of moving averages, Method of least squares.

Time series analysis is done to find out the dynamic conditions for achieving the short-term an long-term goals of business organisations. The past trends from the basis of evaluation the success or failure of the management policies etc. The future patterns can be predicted and policies may accordingly be formulated on the basis of past trends of such organisations. The short-terms and long term factors can also be studied which have effect on the economic and commercial activities in a country. The knowledge of seasonal fluctuations will be of great use for us for taking decisions regarding inventory, production, sales and purchase policies for optimum utilisation of given resources.

CHAPTER 10

Related Literature

A thorough review and survey of related literature is the prerequisite on finally selecting the research topic problem. It is equally important for educators, as it is for others engaged in research, to be able to locate, organise, and use the literature in their field.

Here we have attempted to explain (a) the role of related literature in a research project, (b) reference sources in education, and (c) suggestions on collecting and organising the related literature section of a dissertation.

Related Literature in a Research Project

The search for related literature should be completed before proceeding with the actual conduct of the study. This stage, though if often appears tedious, serves several important functions.

1. *A knowledge of related research enables the investigator to define the frontiers of his field.* To use an analogy, an explorer might say, "We know that beyond this river there are plains for 2000 miles west and beyond those plains a range of mountains, but we do not know what lies beyond the mountains. I propose to cross the plains, go over the mountains, and proceed from there in a westerly direction." So a researcher in a sense says, "The work of A, B, and C has discovered this much about my question; the investigations of D have added this much to our knowledge. I propose to go beyond D's work in the following manner."

2. *An understanding of theory in the field enables the researcher to place his question in perspective.* One should determine whether his endeavors would be likely to add to knowledge in a meaningful way. In general, those studies that determine whether the hypotheses generated by a theory can be confirmed are more useful than studies that proceed completely independent of theory. The latter tend to produce isolated bits of information of limited usefulness.

3. *Through studying related research one learns which procedures and instruments have proved useful and which seem less promising.* As one proceeds through the related literature and develops increasing sophistication, one may soon find oneself seeing ways in which the studies could have been improved. Of course, hindsight is always better than foresight, so perhaps it is inevitable that early studies in a field often seem crude and ineffective. This illustrates a major reason for emphasising the related-literature portion of research studies; both the successes and the failures of past work provide insight for designing one's own study. If researchers build carefully on past investigations, we can expect increasing sophistication in our knowledge about education.

4. *A thorough search through related research avoids unintentional replication of previous studies.* Frequently a researcher develops a worth-while idea only to discover that a very similar study has already been made. In such a case he must decide whether deliberately to replicate the previous work or to change his plans and investigate a different aspect of the problem.

5. *The study of related literature places the researcher in a better position to interpret the significance of his own results.* Becoming familiar with theory in his field and with previous research prepares one for fitting the findings of his research into the body of knowledge in the field.

Reference Sources in Education

It is clearly essential for a scholar or researcher to know how to locate previous work in his area. The main sources of related literature are (1) ERIC, (2) other periodicals, (3) books, (4) dissertations, and (5) information retrieval systems. In order to use the first four of these a scholar needs to familiarise himself with available library facilities. Many libraries have printed guides describing their services and regulations or will schedule orientation tours. It is especially important to learn how the card catalog is organised and how to locate needed periodicals. One should also find out whether the library can obtain books and other documents through interlibrary loan.

Educational Resources Information Center (ERIC)

One of the most important landmarks in the history of educational research was the establishment, in 1964, of the Educational Resources Information Center (ERIC) by the U.S. Office of Education (USOE) to collect, store, and disseminate information on education. The ERIC system has become a vital part of the American educational scene.

The ERIC system is a network of approximately twenty clearing-houses, each devoted to collecting, evaluating, storing, abstracting, and disseminating resource material in its own area of specialisation. (The number of ERIC clearing-houses varies from time to time as the interests and budgets of the USEO change.) The results of this work are made available through the periodicals *Current Index to Journals in Education*[1] and *Research in Education.*[2]

A carefully developed system of indexing is used for classifying ERIC documents. This system has been compiled as the *Thesaurus of ERIC Descriptors,*[3] which is available in most libraries or can be ordered from the CCM Information Corporation. The *ERIC Thesaurus is* a useful source for planning a comprehensive search for related studies in one's area.

Current Index to Journals in Education (CIJE)

The monthly journal *CIJE* is compiled by the specialists of the ERIC clearing-houses. Articles from over 500 journals are classified and listed according to the system developed in the *ERIC Thesaurus.*

CIJE is divided into three sections: (1) subject index, (2) author index, and (3) main entry section. One can locate articles of interest by first looking in the subject index to find the titles and numbers of relevant articles, then using these numbers to locate the entries in the main entry section. If you cannot find your topic of interest in the subject index, look for synonyms for the topic. The vocabulary of the *ERIC Thesaurus* is deliberately limited in order to provide for a more systematic indexing system. If one wishes to find the works of a particular author, he will begin with the author section.

A typical article description taken from the main entry section, with explanation of its various parts, as provided by *CIJE* to illustrate the type of information in each entry.

The annotation is particularly useful, since it gives a brief description of the article. Note that in the example the title alone gives only a partial idea of what the article is about. Before January 1970, when *CIJE* began including annotations, researchers, endured extensive frustration locating articles whose titles were misleading or insufficiently revealing and which on inspection proved to be unrelated to the topic of interest. If the title of an article is considered to be sufficient to convey the main thrust of the article, the *CIJE* staff do not include an annotation. *CIJE* began publication in 1969. It is cumulated semiannually and annually.

An efficient approach to the use of *CIJE* falls into five stages:

1. Determine the key words under which articles relevant to your study might be listed.

2. Begin your search with the most recent issues of *CIJE* and work back through earlier issues.
3. In order to facilitate locating an article, be sure to copy the entire reference given for any title which may be useful.
4. Search out the articles in their journals. If your library does not have the journal, they may be able to obtain a Xerox copy of the article through interlibrary loan.
5. If an abstract is provided with the article, read this first to find out whether it will be necessary to read the entire article. In the absence of an abstract, start with the summary and conclusion section.

Research in Education (RIE)

Abstracts of research reports from sources other than journals are indexed and published monthly by ERIC in *Research in Education.* A semiannual cumulative edition is also published. The sources covered by the specialised clearing-houses include reports of all federally funded educational research, abstracts, pamphlets, curriculum guides, significant papers from the proceedings of learned societies and institutes, bibliographies, exemplary course-related materials, teachers guides and program outlines, as well as various other research proposals and project reports. With such a far-ranging coverage it is clear that the documents in the ERIC collections are of vital interest to practitioners as well as researchers in education. Over 50,000 documents are now included and the collection is growing at a rate of 1000 documents per month.

Each abstract is assigned its own accession number for identification purposes and for ordering copies of publications. Three indexes are provided: author or investigator, institution, and subject. Using the appropriate index one finds the titles of documents and their accession numbers which one then uses to locate the individual abstracts in the document resume section or project resume section of the publication. The document section contains abstracts of reports of completed studies and the project section covers interim reports on ongoing projects. The three separate indexes are provided for each of these two categories. Copies of complete publications are usually only available for items listed in the document section. The Procedure for obtaining such copies is described in each issue of *Research in Education.*

The ERIC Document Collection

Individual Documents can be obtained as required or a standing order may be placed with ERIC to receive all documents as they become available. Many libraries have such an arrangement with ERIC, thus making available to their users the entire document collection in a convenient location.

The documents are available in two forms, hard copy and microfiche. In most libraries microfiche is preferred, as it is less expensive and requires less storage space. The cost of each ERIC document is listed in *RIE* for both microfiche and hard copy.

The microfiche technique is a photographic process that reduces pages of printed test to small images. One 4- by 6-inch microfiche sheet contains up to 60 pages of text. An entire book or an extensive file of reports can be reduced to a few sheets of microfiche. The entire ERIC collection in microfiche occupies the space of about one file cabinet.

A machine called a microfiche reader is required to enlarge the images onto a built-in screen and to allow one to proceed from page image to page image. Most libraries and universities have such equipment available. Since their cost is moderate (from about $75 to $400), even small libraries often have these readers available.

The procedure for using *Research in Education* is similar to that used with *CIJE*. One typically begins with the most recent copy and works backward, looking under the subject or subjects of interest. In many cases the abstract will supply all the information one needs. A listing of all but the most recent ERIC documents in one's area of interest can now be obtained through the School Research Information Service (see page 64), thus avoiding the most tedious part of the search.

All projects funded by the USOE are automatically included in the ERIC system, and complete copies of reports of these projects are available through ERIC. Where publication is first made under copyright privileges, reference is made to the source but copies are not available through ERIC. The same procedures apply in the case of books and other materials prepared for sale. ERIC is invaluable to the field of education because it collects and abstracts, from a wide range of source, relevant material for educational researchers, much of which was previously almost impossible to locate.

The ERIC clearing-houses prepare annotated bibliographies on selected topics. Before preparing your own bibliography it is a good idea to write to the clearing-house dealing with your field of interest to see if the clearing-houses staff already have a bibliography which will be of value to you in preparing your own.

A more complete description of the ERIC system and how to use it will be found in a booklet, *How to Use ERIC*,[4] which is available in many libraries or can be purchased from Superintendent of Documents, U.S. Government Printing Office, Washington, D.C. 20202, at a cost of 35 cents.

The clearing houses of the ERIC network wish to make their collections as comprehen-sive as possible and request educators to submit relevant materials. In *How to Use ERIC* we are urged, "If you have prepared a report, speech or paper which you would like to have considered for national dissemination through ERIC, send one copy to:

ERIC
U.S. Office of Education
400 Maryland Avenue, S.W.
Washington, D.C. 20202

Other Periodicals

Various other periodicals are useful for locating up-to-date information on research, theory, and contemporary opinion in education. These publications, which are issued in successive parts at regular intervals, serve as guides for locating information that is widely dispersed in journals and other sources.

One of the standard reference works in the field of education is the *Education Index,*[5] which has been published regularly by the H.W. Wilson Company of New York since 1929. This publication, which is similar to *CIJE,* though smaller in scope, lists the titles of all articles in more than 200 periodicals, yearbooks, bulletins, proceedings, and monographic series in the field of education.

The procedure for using *Education Index* is similar to that employed in using *CIJE.* However, since annotations are not provided in *Education Index,* one is likely to lose considerable time on occasion locating articles that prove to be unrelated to one's topics. *Education Index* is the best source of locating journal articles prior to the establishment of *CIJE* in 1969.

The *Readers Guide to Periodical Literature,*[6] which has been published by the H.W. Wilson Company since 1900, indexes articles in popular magazines. Prior to the establishment of the *Education Index* in 1929, many education journals were covered in *Readers Guide.* Specialised indexes similar to the *Education Index* are also available for business education, industrial arts, agriculture, and a variety of other fields. These may be of great help to researchers whose topics touch on such fields.

Journals of abstracts are produced in a number of subject areas. Those most likely to be of interest to educators are *Child Development Abstracts and Bibliography*[7] and *Psychological Abstracts.*[8] These publications consist of abstracts of the articles indexed. These abstracts present a clear summary of the content of the article, thus enabling one to determine immediately whether an article is relevant or not.

The *Review of Educational Research,*[9] published by the American Educational Research Association five times each year, summarises research findings in education and related fields. From 1931 until 1970 the *Review* concentrated on one of 15 broad areas within education for each review. An issue chairman was chosen for each topic with the responsibility of soliciting reviews in his area of expertise. Thus, each topic was reviewed once every three years and an educator could depend upon having available relatively recent reviews of research in his field.

In June 1970 the *Review of Educational Research* abandoned this policy and began publishing unsolicited reviews. This means that each issue now contains reviews covering an assortment of topics. The editorial board is planning an *Annual Review of Educational Research* to provide a periodical review of published research classified under broad area headings.

Psychological studies that are also of interest to educators are summarised in the *Annual Review of Psychology.*[10]

Books

Certain books have proven especially useful to those who are engaged in educational research. *Documentation in Education,*[11] by Arvid J. and Mary A. Burke, provides useful and explicit information on how to locate information in our field through references, directories, periodicals, and other sources. *A Guide to Reference Books,*[12] by Constance M. Winchell, describes and evaluates several thousand references. This publication is kept up to date by means of biennial supplements.

Mental Measurements Yearbook,[13] compiled by Oscar K. Buros, is considered the standard reference work on commercially available psychological, educational, and vocational tests. Each volume includes independent evaluation of the tests as well as details concerning publisher, price, and grade level. *Tests in Print: A Comprehensive Bibliography of Tests for Use in Education, Psychology, and Industry,*[14] by the same author, serves as an index and supplement to those volumes of the *Mental Measurements Year- book* which preceded its publication. A revised edition of *Tests in Print* including tests from the recent volumes of *Mental Measurements* is in preparation for publication in 1972. Buros' *Reading Tests and Reviews* lists reading tests and revisions of these tests prior to its publication in 1968. Reviews of tests included in the previous volumes of *Mental Measurements Yearbook* and included, but reviews of tests and revisions published after the sixth yearbook in 1965 are not included. His *Personality Tests and Reviews* lists and describes tests from the first through the sixth yearbooks.[15] Shaw and Wright's *Scales for the Measurement of Attitudes*[16] describes many attitudinal measures, including several that are not available commercially but which may be obtained from the investigators who developed them for their own research.

Carter Good's *Dictionary of Education*[17] provides definitions of over 17,000 terms in the field.

The *Encyclopedia of Educational Research,*[18] a project of the American Educational Research Association, presents useful summaries and evaluations of research in a wide variety of topics in the field of education. New edition is published at the end of each decade. Tne most recent edition was published in 1969 and edited by Robert Ebel.

Sometimes research results are reported in book form. For example, Rosenthal and Jacobson reported their study on teacher expectation as antecedent to pupil achievement in their book, *Pygmalion in the Classroom.*

Dissertations

Dissertation Abstracts, published by University Microfilms, Ann Arbor, Mich., contains abstracts of all doctoral dissertations accepted by over 150 universities in the United States and Canada. These abstracts are classified by subject, institution, and author. *Dissertation Abstracts* is published monthly and indexed annually.

One can seek related dissertations through the same procedure employed in using *CIJE.* If one needs more information than is contained in the abstract,. a microfilm copy of the entire dissertation can be obtained from University Microfilms at a nominal cost.

A more efficient way to find related dissertations is to use the DATRIX service of University Microfilms. DATRIX users fill out a request form on which they identify the relevant dimensions of their question. The information on a completed form enables University Microfilms to identify and provide abstracts of all relevant dissertations through the use of a computer sort. Over 125,000 dissertations are now available through this computer sorting routine. The cost of DATRIX service is modest, especially when compared with the time involved in searching through *Dissertation Abstracts* on one's own.

Since 1962 University Microfilms has also published abstracts of selected masters theses in *Masters Abstracts.* Complete theses in microfilm or Xerox copies can be purchased.

The Phi Delta Kappa's *Research Studies in Education* lists both completed and ongoing dissertations in the field of education classified by subject field. H.M. Silvey's *Master's Theses in Education* lists masters theses from several universities.

Information Retrieval Systems

In view of the accelerating knowledge explosion, it is a blessing that automatic information retrieval systems in the field of education are being developed. These systems make the search for related literature much easier than it was formerly.

School Research Information Service

An example of such a system is the School Research Information Service (SRIS) of Phi Delta Kappa. The type of information gathered by SRIS includes copies of school research reports, descriptions of innovative practices and syllabi, curriculum study results, the complete collection in the USOE storage and retrieval system (ERIC), and many other documents which have not heretofore been readily available. Information is solicited from workers in the field and also supplied by volunteer document locators among the active PDK membership of over 85,000 educators.

Upon receipt of a report the SRIS staff first determine whether it would be of interest to any of the ERIC clearinghouses, in which case it is forwarded to the appropriate clearinghouse and is incorporated into the ERIC system. This is done to avoid duplication of the ERIC services.

Other documents are incorporated into the SRIS collection. The staff determine the key words or retrieval terms under which the document should be listed. The retrieval terms are based on the *ERIC Thesaurus* to insure compatibility between ERIC and SRIS holdings. A number is assigned to each document, and this number is then punched onto subject cards labeled with the appropriate descriptors. These cards are analogous to the librarian's card catalog. From them reports can be selected mechanically, using the descriptors relevant to a request as sorting keys.

SRIS also maintains and encodes the collection of ERIC documents. Therefore, a request to SRIS will not only produce copies of relevant reports in the SRIS system, with abstracts of these reports, but also a list of relevant ERIC document numbers that may be looked up in *Researcher in Education* or ordered directly from the ERIC Document Reproduction Center.

A letter or phone call requesting information is all that is required to make use of the SRIS retrieval service. Bear in mind that the more specifically one details the problem, the easier it will be for the SRIS staff to identify the key words to use in sorting their cards. As an example of how the process works, an account of the handling of the following actual letter has been described by the SRIS staff.

Gentlemen:

> Our school district is presently reevaluating our curriculum, particularly in the area of nongraded classes for elementary schools. Would you please send us any material or research you may have on the subject?
>
> Thank you for your assistance.

After identifying "Curriculum," Elementary Schools," and "Nongraded Classes" as the key words in this question, cards bearing those terms were selected, placed on a "reader," and used to identify documents. This sort located 61 documents indexed under "Curriculum," of which only 24 were related to "Elementary Schools." Of these, only two were also classified under "Nongraded Classes." Thus, in a matter of seconds, the two relevant documents were selected from the thousands in the SRIS holdings. The microfiche masters for these studies were pulled, reproductions made, and sent to the requestor along with copies of their abstracts.

The SRIS service also makes a computer run of the ERIC holdings by descriptor, author, institution, or abstract field, as desired by the client. In like manner another run is made of the listings appearing in the *Current Index to Journals in Education (CIJE).* In both cases a printout of the document abstracts pertinent to the area under investigation is provided for the client.

A nominal fee of $5 is charged for each search. In addition, if the client should require a copy of a microfiche in either the SRIS or the ERIC files, the cost is 25 cents for each copy. In the event of the client seeking a paper copy of an SRIS document, the cost is 10 cents per page. These material costs are over and above the $2 flat rate per individual search.

The identification of relevant documents from the ERIC collection and from *CIJE* is a very important service. Educators now have a quick and relatively inexpensive method for locating relevant documents in their field.

A second and recent feature of the SRIS operation is that of providing selective dissemination. Basically this entails the preparation of bibliographies of ERIC abstracts on a quarterly basis in given areas of study. At the present time two such areas are offered, namely, educational research and evaluation, and foreign language education. However, it is the hope and intention of the center to expand the number of areas covered as soon as the demand warrants it. Proposed additional areas are educational administration, adult education, counseling and guidance, curriculum, educational psychology, and social studies. A number of descriptors pertinent to the area are searched on a regular basis. The subscription fee for this service is $20 per year.

The School Research Information Service also publishes its own quarterly journal, its emphasis being upon the research process. The *SRIS Quarterly*, published in March, June, September, and December, has a subscription rate of $3 per year.

The staff of SRIS urge educators to send them any reports or documents that might be of interest to others. A retrieval service must have a healthy input of documents in order to fulfil its important role of disseminating knowledge in a profession.

Science Information Exchange (SIE)

The Science Information Exchange provides a clearinghouse of information about work currently in progress, classified not only by subject matter but also by location, chief investigators, and source of funding. All fields of behavioral, social, biological, and medical sciences are included, and the research project summaries received each year total over 100,000, about 80 per cent of which are supported by the Federal Government.

One can request current research notices by subject content, by state or country, institution or company, specific school, supporting agency, period of time, individual investigator, or any combination of these. The result of such a request is a list of projects giving complete data plus a 200-word abstract on each project. Fees for this service are based on the type of search required, and the number of abstracts sent.

One can make requests by writing to: Science Information Service, 1730 M Street, N.W. Washington, D.C. 20036, or by telephoning (202) 381-5511 for general information or (202) 381-5721 with inquiries relating to education and other behavioral sciences.

Organising the Related Literature

Once a researcher is satisfied that he has carried out a reasonably comprehensive study of the literature in his field he can proceed to the task of organising it. A useful approach is to arrange the studies by topic and determine how each of these topics relates to one's own study.

The literature should be presented in such a way as to justify carrying out the study by showing what is known and what remains to be investigated in the topic of concern. The hypotheses provide a framework for organising the related literature. Like an explorer proposing an expedition, one maps out the known territory and points the way to the unknown territory he proposes to explore. If the study has several aspects, or is investigating more than a single hypothesis, this is done separately for each facet of the study.

One should avoid the presentation of the literature as a series of abstracts. Rather, it should be presented in such a way as to lay a systematic foundation for the study.

It is almost inevitable that a number of the reports one has carefully studied and included in his notes will on reflection prove to be only peripherally related to the topic. It is neither necessary nor desirable to include in a proposal every study encountered in a search through the literature. One's readers with not be impressed by mere quantity. Relevance and organisation of the material is of prime importance.

Some Tips on Organising Notes

Unless the researcher approaches the task of assembling the related literature in a systematic manner from the beginning, he can become very disorganised. The following suggestions may be of assistance.

1. *Begin with the most recent studies in your field and then work backward through earlier volumes.* One obvious advantage of this approach is that you start with studies that have already incorporated the thoughts and findings of previous research. Earlier misunderstandings have been corrected and unprofitable approaches have been avoided. Another advantage is that these studies will include references to earlier works and, therefore, direct you to sources you might not otherwise encounter. In fact, accumulating a network of references in this way is rather like pulling up crabgrass. As you pull out one, its roots lead you to others that when pulled out lead you to still others, *ad nauseam!* Obviously, limits must be set to the process of gathering related research. On the one hand, laying a meaningful groundwork for a study entails including all the important works in the field.

On the other hand, devoting excessive time to this endeavor could result in boring the readers of your own report with superfluous detail. Make sure that the related literature serves, but does not dominate, your own work.

2. *Read the abstract or summary section of a report first to determine whether it is relevant to your question.* This can save much time that might be wasted reading unhelpful articles.

3. *Before taking notes skim the report quickly to find those sections that are related to your question.* This is another way to save reading time.

4. *Make notes directly on file cards as they are easier to sort and organise than sheets of paper, backs of envelopes, and so on.* Many prefer 4- by 6-inch file cards, which provide a reasonable space for notes but are small enough to fit a pocket or purse.

5. *For each work write out the complete bibliographic reference.* If you know which style manual will be used in the finished report, you can save time by using that reference form while note-taking. Add the library call number, also. This will facilitate finding the work again, should it be necessary.

6. *To facilitate sorting and organising do not put more than one reference on each card.* It is not possible to arrange your references alphabetically or in any other way unless you record them singly.

7. *Be sure to indicate which parts of the notes are direct quotations from the author and which are your own paraphrases.* Failure to make this distinction can lead to inadvertent plagiarism. It is also wise to clearly separate an author's evaluation of his research from your own.

TABLE 1

Sources of Related Literature in Education

Source	*Content*
Current Index to Journals in Education	Titles, authors, and journal citations of journal articles related to education, with annotations where needed. Classification by subject and by author. No abstracts.
Research in Education	Documents section: Abstracts of completed research and other documents acquired by ERIC clearinghouses. Projects section: Abstracts of ongoing projects compiled by ERIC clearinghouses.
Thesaurus of ERIC Descriptors	System for classifying and indexing ERIC documents.
ERIC Microfiche Collection	Complete documents, the abstracts of which are in the *Research in Education* documents section (where available).
Education Index	Titles, authors, and journal citations of journal articles related to education. Indexed by subject and title. No abstracts.
Readers Guide to Periodical Literature	Titles, authors, and journal citations of articles in popular journals. Indexed by subject and title. No abstracts.
Child Development Abstracts and Bibliography	Abstracts of journal articles in the field of child development.
Psychological Abstracts	Abstracts of journal articles in psychology.
Review of Educational Research	Before June 1970: Review of research in selected topics in education in a three-year cycle. Beginning June 1970: Unsolicited reviews in various topics in each issue.
Encyclopedia of Educational Research	Summaries and Evaluations of research in education, published at the end of each decade.
Dissertation Abstracts	Abstracts of doctoral dissertations in the United States and Canada.
DATRIX	Computerised sorting system for locating relevant dissertations listed in *Dissertation Abstracts.*
Mental Measurements Yearbooks	Information and evaluations of commercially available tests.
Tests in Print	Index and supplement to *Mental Measurements Yearbooks* before 1961.
Scales for the Measurement of Attitude	Describes and illustrates attitudinal measures not listed in the *Mental Measurements Yearbooks.*

Summing Up

If the compiler-researcher covers the avenues to information in his area as suggested, he should have a complete picture of the place his study occupies within his field.

Table 1 explains the most important sources of related literature in education and their content.

REFERENCES

1. *Current Index to Journals in Education*, CCM Information Corpn., 866, Third Avenue, New York, N.Y. 10022.
2. *Research in Education*, Superintendent of Documents, U.S. Government Printing Office, Washington, D.C. 20402.
3. *Thesaurus of ERIC Descriptors*. CCM Information Corporation, 866 Third Avenue, New York, N.Y. 10022, 1970.
4. U.S. Department of Health, Education and Welfare, *How to Use ERIC* (Washington, D.C., 1970).
5. *Education Index*, (New York: H.W. Wilson, 1929-date).
6. *Readers Guide to Periodical Literature* (New York: H.W. Wilson, 1900-date).
7. *Child Development Abstracts and Bibliography* (Washington: National Research Council, 1927-date).
8. *Psychological Abstracts* (Lancaster, Pa.: American Psychological Association, 1927-date).
9. *Review of Educational Research* (Washington: American Educational Research Association, 1931-date).
10. *Annual Review of Psychology* (Palo Alto, Calif.: Annual Reviews Inc., 1950-date).
11. Arvid J. Burke and Mary A. Burke, *Documentation in Education* (New York: Teachers College Press, Columbia University, 1967).
12. Constance M. Winchell (ed.), *A Guide to Reference Books* (Chicago: American Library Association, 1967).
13. O.K. Buros, *Mental Measurements Yearbook* (Highland Park, N.J.: Gryphon, Vol. 1, 1938; Vol. 2, 1940; Vol. 3, 1949; Vol. 4, 1953; Vol. 5, 1959; Vol. 6, 1965; Vol. 7, 1972).
14. O.K. Buros, *Tests in Print: A Comprehensive Bibliography of Tests for Use in Education, Psychology, and Industry* (Highland Park, N.J.: Gryphon, 1961).

15. O.K. Buros, *Reading Tests and Reviews* (Highland Park, N.J.: Gryphon, 1968); *Personality Tests and Reviews* (Highland Park, N.J.: Gryphon, 1971).
16. Marvin E. Shaw and Jack M. Wright, *Scales for the Measurement of Attitudes* (New York: McGraw-Hill, 1967).
17. Carter V. Good, ed., *Dictionary of Education* (New York: McGraw-Hill, 1959).
18. Robert Ebel (ed.), *Encyclopedia of Educational Research*, American Educational Research Association (New York: Macmillan, 1969).

CHAPTER 11

Writing Research Proposals: Technique & Guidelines

Presentation of the research report in an excellent way is the key problem on completion of a research through conventionally dissertations and reports are presented in a routined way. Every budding research wishes to present his report in some unique form.

Writing the research report is the most crucial and exciting stagein the research process. At this stage the whole project crystallises into concrete form. In the proposal the researcher demonstrates that he knows what he is seeking, how he will see it if it is there, and why the search is worthwhile. This may be the relatively informal outline offered by a student to satisfy the requirements of an introduction to research class, a formal thesis of dissertation proposal presented to a committee, or a funding request to a foundation or governmental agency.

The following nine categories of information should appear in dissertations:

1. Statement of the problem.
2. Review of the literature.
3. Hypotheses.
4. Instrumentation.
5. Sampling.
6. Design.
7. Data collection and statistical procedures.

8. Significance.
9. Budget and time schedule.

Although it is not necessary to follow this list rigidly, it should provide a useful outline for the writing of any proposal. A careful consideration of each category is needed in writing a proposal.

1. Statement of the Problem

A clear and direct statement of the problem should be made very early in the proposal, ideally at the beginning of the first paragraph, followed by a description of the background of the question. This section of the proposal should also include a brief indication of the potential significance of the study, although it is important to avoid the temptation to sell the importance of the topic before stating it. Two common errors to watch for are: (1) beginning a proposal with an elaborate laying out of the background of a problem before clearly stating the problem itself and (2) presenting a justification for the study with the statement of the problem buried in the discussion or only vaguely brought in near the end.

Usually the background of one's problem will be developed in the section on related literature. However, it is sometimes appropriate to mention in the statement of the problem those studies that have led directly to it.

At an appropriate point in this section, any terms that may not be familiar to the reader or those to which the author is ascribing specific meanings in his study should be defined in the way they will be used in the study. The specific limitations of the scope of the study and a foreshadowing of the hypothesis should close this section.

2. Review of the Literature

In the section on related literature one portrays what is so far known about the problem under consideration. This provides the setting for the questions or hypotheses of the proposed study. The U.S. Office of Education advises proposal writers, "Tie the relevant literature to the objectives of the proposed study. The literature does not have to be exhaustive, but should contain the most pertinent related studies and show an awareness of promising current practices."

In this section the writer not only demonstrates how he proposes to proceed from the known to the unknown but also demonstrates his grasp of the field and his awareness of recent developments. This does not mean that this should be a tour de force of one's erudition. Only literature that clearly relates to the objectives of one's study should be included.

The literature should be organised by topic. Such an organisation serves to point out to the reader what is known about various aspects of the study. Thus, a complete picture of the background of one's study is put together step by step.

A pitfall to be avoided in a related literature section is the presentation of a series of abstracts, one per paragraph. By doing this, the author presents his audience with tedious reading and misses the opportunity for laying meaningful groundwork for his study. It is much better to organise by topic and to point out how the studies presented relate to one's question or questions.

In reviewing several similar studies, the author may describe the most important one, them simply state that the results were confirmed in similar studies that are listed but are not described in detail. Enthusiastic beginning researchers often imagine their proposed study is unique and that there is no related research available. This is very rarely the case. A thorough search will almost always turn up several research papers related to at least some aspect of one's study. Even if there should chance to be no research in the field, there is usually literature of a theoretical or speculative nature that should be included as part of the background of a study. The related literature section should conclude with a discussion of the findings and their implications. Here the author shares the insights he has gained from the review of the literature and points out the gaps presently existing in what a known about his topic, and thus leads directly to the question he proposes to investigate.

3. Hypotheses

The problem, which has already been stated in a general way, should now be made specific. If the project is a survey, the problem will be stated in question from.

If the project is designed to test a theory, however, the problem will be stated in hypothesis form; for example, "The chemistry achievement of students who have used the Chemical Bond Approach materials in a chemistry course will be superior to the achievement of those students who have taken a more traditional course in chemistry."

Although the answer to a survey question may take any number of values, the answer to a hypothesis-testing experiment is always either yes or no.

The statement of the research hypothesis typically is determined by the implications of the related literature and the deductive logic of the study. In the chemistry example given above one would assume that previous research or theory led the researcher to expect that students using the Chemical Bond Approach would learn more than those using another method. Therefore, the researcher states in his hypothesis the expectation that the scores of the experimental group will exceed those of the control group.

Some authorities suggest that the hypothesis should be stated in null form since it is the null hypothesis that will be involved in the statistical test. However, we suggest that in this section of the proposal a research hypothesis be stated in terms of anticipated relationships between variables. In this way the author gives his readers a clearer indication of the intent of the study than would be conveyed if the null hypothesis were stated at this point. The use of the research hypothesis at this stage also allows the researcher to build the deductive logic underlying his study.

Although the hypothesis may be introduced in a general form, it is necessary that the operational definition of each element within the hypothesis be included at this point in the proposal. In the present example, the proposer would need to define chemistry achievement operationally, and to stipulate what he means by student, Chemical Bond Approach, and traditional chemistry courses. This hypothesis in such form might read, *"The ACS-NSTA Cooperative Examination: High School Chemistry* test scores of beginning high school chemistry students who have been instructed for one year from the Chemical Bond Approach course outline in the manner described in *Chemical Systems* will exceed the scores of an equivalent class taught for the same period of time according to the procedures described in the *Teacher's Guide to the Modern Chemistry Programme* test.

It is convenient if a hypothesis can be stated concisely in operational form. If this is not possible, a hypothesis stated in general terms should be followed by the definitions and stipulations necessary to define the hypothesis in operational form.

4. Instrumentation

The goal of a research project is to investigate relationships between constructs. However, since constructs are usually impossible to measure directly we must select or develop indicators that will approximate them as well as possible. In our example, the constructs of interest are method of teaching and chemistry achievement. We actively manipulate the independent variable, method of teaching, and measure the dependent variable, chemistry achievement. Since we cannot measure chemistry achievement directly, the *ACS-NSTA*

Cooperative Examination: High School Chemistry has been chosen as the indicator of this construct. The methods of teaching are operationally defined by the procedures given in the teacher's guides.

Inasmuch as the instruments used will provide the operational definition of the variables, their use must be justified as being appropriate for that purpose. In the example under consideration, the criterion is not, strictly speaking, achievement in chemistry but rather scores on the ASC-NSTA test. The proposal should explain why the instrument used was selected as the most appropriate definition of the variable under consideration.

If an instrument is one already established, the proposal should include reported evidence of its reliability and also its validity for the purpose of the study. If the researcher is developing his own instruments, he should outline the procedure to be followed in their development. If this results in so much detail that it interrupts the continuity of the proposal, one may prefer to include such detail in an appendix rather than in the text.

5. Sampling

The sampling procedure defines the population from which one will draw the subjects and the procedure to be used to select these subjects.

In terms of statistical inference, the results of an experiment can be generalised only to the population from which the subjects were randomly selected. In order to indicate the potential external validity of a study to the reader, the population and the sampling procedure should be carefully described.

6. The Design

In the design section one describes how one will set up one's experiment in such a way that the hypothesised relationships will be observed if these relationships do in fact exist. In effect the researcher is saying "*If* this hypothesis is true *then* these results will be observe." In our example, *if* a relation exists between method of teaching chemistry and student proficiency in chemistry *then* when groups of students of equivalent ability are taught by different methods under conditions that are otherwise identical, one should observe different mean chemistry proficiency scores between the groups at the conclusion of the experiment. By designing the study explicitly as an operation to permit the observation of the hypothesised relationships, the researcher lays the foundation for his study.

In the design section the steps that will be taken to answer the questions and test and hypotheses are specified. The designation of these steps should be complete and in operational form. By basing the design on the hypotheses, one facilitates direct and unambiguous interpretation of results. Researchers are often tempted to collect additional data that are not directly related to the hypotheses. This practice may sometimes be profitable, but it often leads to results that are very difficult to interpret.

A useful procedure is fist to picture what the criterion scores or results are likely to be. In the example, these would be the ACS-NSTA test scores for the control and experimental groups. These scores are interval measures and will permit the use of interval statistics for analysing the data.

Then one should consider possible confounding variables, those variables that could account for criterion score differences that are not part of the independent variable. In the example under discussion, student ability, motivation, previous experience, teacher ability. time spent in chemistry class, physical setting, and laboratory facilities of the two groups would be among the possible confounding variables. The design should specify how one proposes to control for these variables. For example, one might control for student and teacher differences by random assignment of students and teachers to the control and experimental groups. The time spent, physical setting, and laboratory facilities could be made equivalent. After the design section has been drafted, it should be reread to verify that all steps necessary to answer *every* question and test *every* hypothesis have been described.

7. Data Collection and Statistical Procedures

The design of the study determines what statistical techniques should be employed, not vice versa. In other words, one decides what design will enable him to observe the hypothesised relationships, then one selects the statistical procedure that fits the questions asked and the nature of the data involved. One does not first select an appealing statistic and then design the study to fit the statistic.

The appropriate statistic to use is determined partly by the type of measurement scale characterising the dependent variable. Therefore, the rows in the table are identified as interval, ordinal, and nominal. The columns list the various purposes descriptive statistics may serve.

The required cell can be located by identifying the row and column heading appropriate to one's study. Each cell is divided and the section to use is determined by whether one's study is concerned with one group or with more than one group. (Recall that one *may* choose a statistic for a lower scale of measurement but not the reverse; for example, one may use a median or a mode to describe interval data but may not use a mean to describe ordinal or nominal data.)

In determining what type of scale to use in expressing the data one should consider the advantages of all three scales on the descriptive level. Interval data typically provide more information than ordinal data and ordinal data provide more information than nominal data. In making inferences, statistical tests of interval data are more "powerful" than tests of ordinal data; that is, one has a greater chance of rejecting a null hypothesis when interval measures are used than when ordinal measures are used. In the same manner, ordinal tests are more powerful than nominal measures. Therefore, when a choice is possible, a researcher will prefer interval data to ordinal and ordinal to nominal.

In our example we have interval data for the dependent variable; therefore, we want an index to describe the difference between groups. The table identifies the difference between two means as an appropriate statistics. It should be remembered that a statistic is selected on the basis of appropriateness for answering the question involved in the study. Nothing is gained by using a complicated statistic when a simple one will do just as well. Statistics are to serve research, not to dominate it.

A compact description of the plans for administering the instruments and collecting the data should be given. These plans should include the time schedule, procedures for replacing subjects lost during the course of the experiment, plans for counterbalancing for order effects if needed, and other necessary details.

8. Significance

Since the research is aimed at increasing knowledge level, the proposal writer should show how his study will do this. It is also appropriate to suggest how such an extension of knowledge may improve educational practices. In addition, the proposal writer may explain how this own experience and expertise, coupled with the facilities and goals of his institution, place him in a favourable position to solve the problem in question.

9. Budget and Time Schedule

Reviewing the previous sections of the proposal, the researcher now lists the personnel, equipment, space, and time that will be required for the project. Most universities and school systems have an agency responsible for assisting in the preparation of research budgets. Such an agency gives advice concerning the local and agency regulations and procedures and can assist in translating the needs of one's proposal into dollars-and-cents figures. The researcher should also prepare a realistic schedule for completing the research within the time available.

CRITIQUING PROPOSALS

After completing the draft of a proposal, one should go through it again carefully with a critical eye. It is also profitable to have one's colleagues read one's proposal. Often a colleague can identify weaknesses or omissions that are not evident to the author.

Smith in his work with the Research Advisory Committee of the USOE Cooperative Research Programme identified six common weaknesses that the committee found in proposals submitted for funding. The are:

The Problem is Trivial: Problems that are of only peripheral interest to educators or show little likelihood of adding to knowledge in education are not considered to be deserving of support. Smith gives as an example a plan to study an adult education programme for library trustees and comments. "Not only is it of peripheral value to education and oriented toward action rather than research, but it is, to put it bluntly, a problem of little significance."

The Problem is Not Delimited: The classic illustration by Good and Skates is a splendid example of this weakness. A letter written by a graduate student to the Commissioner of Education for Alaska indicated that the student had selected for his thesis the topic "The teaching of English as Revealed in the Courses of Study of the English-Speaking Nations of the World." In the second paragraph, he asks the commissioner, "Do you know some interesting books on Alaska: her history, her economic problems, commerce, imports, exports, human relations, religion, etc...." In order to produce a feasible proposal, one must focus one's study. This is not to say that a study should never include a number of related variables. One should attack those aspects of a problem which can reasonably be handled in a single study.

The Objectives, Hypotheses, or Questions are Stated too Broadly: Proposal writers are often tempted to state their objectives, hypotheses, or questions in broad, sweeping generalisations. In such cases one finds when reading the procedures section that the actual planned study is not capable of meeting the grand objectives set forth. Sometimes the objectives or hypotheses are stated in such broad, general terms that one must go to the procedures to discover what the study is really about. It seems obvious that the objectives and procedures should match; yet the Research Advisory Committee found this lacking in many proposals.

The Procedures are Lacking in Detail: Smith points out "An investigator who omits more than he includes should not expect the committee to read procedural details between the lines. The committee lacks both the desire and the clairvoyance to do so." Remember, the procedures should be complete enough to allow for replication.

A Simple Design is Used to Investigate a Complex Problem: The design of a study should fit the problem. A simple comparison of the means of two groups is appropriate when a single variable is involved. More complex studies require more complex designs.

Relevant Variables are Not Considered or are Lightly Dismissed: Failure to consider relevant extraneous variables is a serious error in a research proposal. An investigator should demonstrate that he is aware of such variables and explain how he will handle them in his design.

Completing the Proposal Before Collecting Data

A clear, well-stated, complete proposal indicates that the prospective researcher is actually ready to set his study in motion. It shows that he knows what to do, why to do it, and how to do it. If the prospective researcher cannot produce a complete and coherent proposal, clearly he is not yet ready to proceed to the data-collecting stage of his project. Novice researchers are ofttimes inclined to say, "Let me collect my data now and decide what to do with it later." Simultaneously collecting data and writing the proposal may sound like a time-saving procedure, but such is seldom the case. Countless man-hours and thousands of dollars have been wasted in just that way. Until the proposal is formulated, one cannot be sure exactly what data will be needed, nor what will be the best way to handle this information in the light of the purpose of the study. Those working under deadlines should set for themselves a date for the completion of the proposal well in advance of the target date for completing the entire project.

Summary and Conclusion

There are several aspects of the research proposal that are especially important in laying the foundation for the interpretation of the results. The first of these is an explicit and direct statement of the problem. In the statement of the problem, clear and unambiguous definition of the variables is essential. If the variables of the study are poorly defined, the results of the study will be vague. Consequently, the clarity of the definitions of the variables sets an upper limit to the clarity of the results of the study.

In the writing of the related literature section, the researcher facilitates the interpretation of his results by building the theoretical framework within they will be interpreted. He also describes the results of other studies and the interpretations given to these results.

The theoretical base for interpreting the results of the study should be completed in the question sand/or hypothesis section of the project. In this section one employe deductive logic to predict the outcomes of the study and fit the expected outcomes into the framework provided by theory in the field and by the results of previous studies.

In the design section one determines how to order the data in such a manner as to demonstrate best the meaning of the observations. By basing the design on the hypothesis, one facilitates the interpretation of the results and provides the basis for determining their statistical significance. One provides design that will allow the hypothesised state of affairs to appear in the data if this state of affairs does in fact exist.

The data in a study do not directly indicate a relationship between one construct and another, but only a relationship between measures. A study of the relationship between intelligence and arithmetic achievement, for example, does not directly related these two constructs. Rather it infers a relationship between them from an observed relationship between intelligence test scores and arithmetic achievement test scores. In the instrumentation section, one justifies the instruments used in the study as legitimate operational definitions of the constructs involved.

In the sampling section, the researcher identifies the population about which he wishes to make statements and devises a sampling system that will justify interpretation of the data in the context of that population.

The proposal should include a section on the potential significance of the study that draws the previous elements together and shows how the study should add to the body of knowledge in education. Finally, the manpower and money resources needed are identified in the budget and time schedule.

Thus, following these guidelines will help an investigator produce his report in a presentable way. One should remember the distinction between the research and criticism.

Select Bibliography

Argyris, Chris, "Some Problems in Conceptualizing Organizational Climate: A Case Study of a Bank," *Administrative Science Quarterly*, 2 1958: 501-520.

Arvid J. Burke and Mary A. Burke, *Documentation in Education* (New York: Teachers College Press, Columbia University, 1967).

Backstrom, Charles H., and Gerald D. Hursh, *Survey Research*, Evanston, Ill: Northwestern University Press, 1963.

Carter V. Good, ed., *Dictionary of Education*, (New York: McGraw-Hill, 1959).

Carter V. Good and Douglas E. Skates, *Methods of Research* (New York: Appleton, 1954).

Champion, Dean J., and Edward Z. Dager, "Some Impacts of Office Automation upon Status, Role Change, and Depersonalization," Sociological Quarterly, 8 1967: 71-84.

Chemical Bond Approach Project, *Chemical Systems* (New York: McGraw-Hill, 1964).

Chinoy, Ely, Automobile Workers and the American Dream. Garden City, N.Y.: Doubleday, 1955.

Clausen, Aage R., "Response Validity in Surveys," *Public Opinion Quarterly*, 32 1969: 588-606.

Constance M. Winchell (ed.), *A Guide to Reference Books* (Chicago: American Library Association, 1967).

Davis, Fred, "The Cabdriver and His Fare: Facets of a Fleeting Relationship," *American Journal of Sociology*, 65 1959: 158-165.

Dean, John P., and William Foote Whyte, "How do you Know if the Informant is Telling the Truth?," *Human Organization*, 17, 1958: 34-38.

Egon Guba, "Guides for the Writing of Proposals," in Jack A. Culbertson and Stephen P. Hencly (eds.) *Educational Research: New Perspectives* (Danville, Ill.: Interstate Printers and Publishers, 1963).

Gerald R. Smith, "A Critique of Proposals Submitted to the Cooperative Research Programme," in Jack A. Culbertson and Stephen P. Hencly (eds.), *Educational Research: New Perspectives* (Danville, Ill.: Interstate Printers and Publishers, 1963), Chapter 17.

Goode, William J., and Paul K. Hatt, *Methods in Social Research.* New York: McGraw-Hill, 1952.

Hagedorn, Robert, and Sanford Labovitz, *Introduction to Social Research.* New York: McGraw-Hill, 1971.

H.C. Metcalfe et al., *Teacher's Guide to the Modern Chemistry Programme* (New York: Holt, Rinehart and Winston, 1966).

Hyman, Herbert, *Survey Design and Analysis.* Glencoe, Ill.: The Free Press, 1955.

Kirk, Roger E., *Experimental Design: Procedures for the Behavioral Sciences.* Belmont Calif.: Brooks/Cole Publishing Co., 1968.

Marvin E. Shaw and Jack M. Wright, *Scales for the Measurement of Attitudes* (New York: McGraw-Hill, 1967).

O.K. Buros, *Mental Measurements Yearbook* (Highland Park, N.J.: Gryphon, Vol. 1, 1938; Vol. 2, 1940; Vol. 3, 1949; Vol. 4, 1953; Vol. 5, 1959; Vol. 6, 1965; Vol. 7, 1972).

O.K. Buros, *Reading Tests and Reviews* (Highland Park, N.J.: Gryphon, 1968); *Personality Tests and Reviews* (Highland Park, N.J.: Gryphon, 1971).

Robert Ebel (ed.), *Encyclopedia of Educational Research,* American Educational Research Association (New York: Macmillan, 1969)

Selltiz, Clarie, Marie Jahoda, Morton Deutsch, and Stuart W. Cook. *Research Methods in Social Relations.* New York: Holt, 1959.

Sewell, William H., and Vimal P. Shah, "Social Class, Parental Encouragement, and Educational Aspirations," American Journal of Sociology, 73 1968: 559-572.

U.S. Department of Health, Education and Welfare, *How to Use ERIC* (Washington, D.C., 1970).

U.S. Department of Health, Education, and Welfare, "Small Project Research" (Washington, D.C.: Bureau of Research, U.S. Office of Education, 1966).

White, Lynn C., "Maternal Employment and Anxiety Over Mother Roles," *L.S.U. Journal of Sociology*, 2 1972: 61-81.

Whyte, William Foote, *Human Relations in the Restaurant Industry*. New York: McGraw-Hill, 1948.

Index

A

Adam Smith, 2
Administration Science Quarterly, 77
American Economic Review, 19, 79
American Journal of Sociology, 77
American Sociological Review, 77
Analogies, 33
Anderson, 44
Annual Review of Educational Research, 238
Annual Review of Psychology, 238
ANOVA, 225
Argyris, 55
Attributes,
  association of, 219

B

Barr, A.S., 95, 104, 105
Before-after design, 65
Behavioural Statement Scale, 109
Blackstorm, 47, 48
Burke, Mary A., 238
Buros, Oscar K., 239

C

Case study deign, 53
  major advantages of, 55
  major disadvantages of, 56
  note on, 57
Champion, 44, 53, 78
Chave, 114
Check-list, 102
  analysis and interpretation of data, 104
  guidelines for constructing, 103
Chinoy, Ely, 54
CIJE, 233, 237, 242
Classes,
  limits, 190
  no. of and magnitude, 189
Classical experimental design, 59
Clausen, Aage R., 52
Coding, 187
Control groups, 58
Culture, 33

D

Dager, 53, 54, 75
Data,

degree of accuracy, 161
editing, 184
interpretation and analysis of, 184-229
methods of collecting
primary, 161
direct personal interview, 162
indirect personal interview, 163
methods of collection, 161
prerequisites for collection, 155
information source, 157
scope & objectives of enquiry, 155
statistical units, 156
types of, 157
primary and secondary, 153
selection of, 153
statistical analysis of, 197
Davis, 44, 95, 104
Deviation,
average/mean, 206
standard, 207
Dewey, John, 8
Dictionary of Education, 239
Dispersion, 204
measure of, 204
Dissertation Abstracts International, 15
Dissertation Abstracts, 19, 240
Dubin, 32
Durkheim, 28

E

EDP, 54
Education,
reference sources in, 232
Education Index, 237
Elhance, D.N. (Prof.), 184, 204, 213
Encyclopaedia Educational Research, 239
Encyclopaedia of Social Science Research, 15
ERIC, 232
document collection, 235
ERIC Thesaurus, 241
Experimental design, 58

F

Findikyan, 44
Fisher, R.N., 225
Foreman, 53

G

Garrett, H.E., 37
Good, 107
Goode, William J., 23, 24, 62, 63, 64, 95, 101, 187
Group distribution mathcing, 61, 80
Guttman Scaling, 121
advantages and disadvantages, 122
steps, 118
Guttman, Louis, 121

H

Hagedorn, 53
Hatt, 23, 24, 62, 63, 64, 95, 101, 187
Homer, 103
How to Use ERIC, 236
Hursh, 47
Hyman, 53, 47
Hypothesis, 23-39, 72
charactristics of, 23

characteristics of a usable, 25
different forms of, 35
declaration form, 36
prediction form, 36
question form, 36
difficulties in formulation of, 36
importance of, 34
source, 27
testing, 38
types, 28
use of in different types of research, 26
utility, 25

I

Index Numbers, 222
Individual mathcing, 56
Information retrieval systems, 241
Interview schedules, 121-152
contents of, 131
ediging of, 148
general form and layour of, 129
kinds of, 121
language, 137
limitations, 151
merits of interviews through, 149
nature of questions, 134
organising interviews, 139
pilot studeis and pretests, 137
procedure for farming, 124
purpose of, 122
questions to be avoided, 132
salient features of, 123
sequence of questions, 136
types of questions, 126
ambigous, 128
dichotomous, 127
leading, 128
multiple choice, 127
open-end, 126
ranking item, 128
structural, 126
IQ, 60, 61

J

Johnson, 95
Jacobson, 240
Johnson, Palmer O., 23

K

Kempfer, 106
Kenneys, 117
Keynes, 2

L

Likert method, 117
Likert scaling,
limitations, 117
procedure for, 117, 118
Likert, 114, 121
Lobowitz, 53
Lundberg, 23
Lynds, 54, 55

M

Marx, 28
McCormicks, 44
Mean,
geometric, 202
harmonic, 203
Median, 200
Mental Measurements Yearbook, 239
Merton, 8, 11
Mode, 201
Morris, 44

N

Nieswanger, W.A., 177
Nelson, 44

O

Opinionnarie/Attitude scale, 111
characteristics of, 112
guidelines for preparing, 119
limitations of, 112
Osgood, 117

P

Pearson, Karl, 210, 212, 214, 215, 221
Pilot study, 77
specific functions, of 73
Popper, Karl, 38
Processing,
problems of, 195
Pygmalion in the Classroom, 240

Q

Question,
originating, 9, 10
Rationale of, 8
specifying, 11
Questionnaire, 95
advantages, 100
construction and design, 163
development of, 174
forms of, 96
closed vs. open, 96
fact and opinion, 96
structured vs. non-structured, 96
guidelines of construction of, 98
limitation, 100
salient features of, 97
types of, 170

R

Randon assignment, 56
Range, 204
inter-quartile, 205
semi-interquartile, 205
Rao, C.H. Hanumantha, 32
Rating scale, 104
advantages, 106
common errors in, 108
definition, 104
guidelines for construction and use of, 107
limitations, 106
types, 109
Readers Guide to Periodical Literature, 237
Regression, 216, 217, 218
Related Literature, 230-249, 251
in a research project, 230
organisation of, 244
source of in education of, 247
Relationship,
measures of, 212
Relative Frequency Approach, 227
Research design, 41, 82
after-only design, 63
basic outlines of, 65
conventional types, 47
major functions of, 41
objectives, 42
descriptive, 44
experimental, 445
exploratory, 43
Research in Education (RIE), 234, 235
Research problem, 1-18
common errors, 17
criteria, 4
formulating and stating, 15
formulation, 7
justification of, 17
necessary conditions for formulation of, 12
personal consideration of scholar, 6
selection of, 2
source of, 3

Research proposals,
basic outline for, 66
critique, 259
writing techniques, 250-262
Research subject,
selection of, 79, 82
Research tools, 94-120
inquiry forms, 94
Review of Educational Research, 238

S

Sample design, 83-93
objectives, 84
salient features of good, 86
steps, 84-
budgetary provision, 86
organisation of data, 86
parameters of interest, 85
sampling procedure, 86
sampling unit, 85
size of sample, 85
source list, 85
universe types, 84
types of, 87
cluster, 89
convenience, 92
incidental, 91
judgements, 92
purposive, 92
quota, 91
self-selected, 92
sequential, 93
simple random, 88
stratified rendom, 89
systematic, 91
Sayles, 54
Scates, 104
Schedule, 101
Score card, 110
limitations of, 110
Sears, 78
Secondary data, 177
precaution in use of, 181
sources of, 178
Selltiz, 42, 45, 61, 184
Semantic Differential Method, 117
Shah, 49
SIE, 244
Skewness,
measures of, 209
Social Forces, 77
Social research,
data collection for, 153-183
SRIS Quarterly, 243
Statistical unit,
requirements of, 158
types of, 159
units of analysis, 160
units of collection, 159
Suci, 117
Survey design, 43
general disadvantages of, 51
major advantages of, 50

T

Tabulation,
rules of, 194
types of, 192
higher order, 195
one-way, 193
two way, 193
three way, 193
Tannenbaum, 117
Tests in Print, 239
Thurstone technique of scaled values, 113
Thurstone, 114, 117
Time Series Analysis, 228

U

United States Library of
Congress, 19, 79

US Department of Defence, 75

USOE, 236

V

Van Dalen, 104

W

Wanger, Neis, 192

Washington, 49

White, 49

Winer, 66

Wisconsin, 49

Woodworth, R.S., 1

Y

Ya Lun Chow, 213, 216

Young, P.V., 123, 127

❑❑❑